School Discipline

A whole-school practical approach

Chris Watkins and Patsy Wagner

Basil Blackwell

First published 1987

© Chris Watkins and Patsy Wagner 1987

Reprinted 1988

Published by Basil Blackwell Ltd
108 Cowley Road
Oxford OX4 1JF
England

British Library Cataloguing in Publication Data

Watkins, Chris
School Discipline
(Blackwell studies in personal & social education & pastoral care)
1.
I. Title   II. Wagner, Patsy

ISBN 0–631–14215–0 (pb)
ISBN 0–631–14214–2 (hb)

Typeset in 10½ on 12½ Plantin by Columns of Reading
Printed by T.J. Press Ltd, Cornwall

To
all those we have taught,
all those who have taught us,
and especially those who were both

Contents

Introduction

Why another book on school discipline?

There seem to be about two new books a month on school discipline. Perhaps that indicates the degree of concern which is felt about the topic. But we find many of these offerings disappointing for a range of reasons. Some are written by social scientists who are primarily interested in explanations, and others are written by teachers who are interested in solutions to problems. There is a seldom-bridged gap between the two.

In this volume we intend to present at three main levels potential explanations which are useful to teachers, together with practical strategies which develop from them. In so doing we intend to avoid simple or single or sensational explanations for a multi-faceted topic which surfaces in very different ways in such complex places as schools.

What is this book complaining about?

The first complaint is that many explanations of indisciplined behaviour suggest rather too swiftly that the cause lies somehow within the pupil or their family and background. The result is that other facets or potential causes are left unconsidered, particularly those within the school context. Thus, teachers themselves are left out of the picture and are (unwittingly) made powerless to influence the picture. We believe that this process of locating causes within pupils reflects the lack of attention given to the wider patterns in the behaviours which cause concern.

The second complaint involves the pastoral care system of the school. In too many schools pastoral care is distorted into an unproductive system supposed to deal with the immediate manifestations of indiscipline. We regard this as a serious potential failure of pastoral care (see also Hamblin, 1986): it is short-term, reactive, distorts the roles of pastoral staff and others, and considerably sells short the pupils' personal, intellectual and social development, which is the responsibility of all teachers and which the pastoral care system was devised to encourage. We do not ascribe a simple cause or blame for this state of affairs, but consider it open to influence by pastoral staff and the school system at large.

What does this book offer?

It offers all teachers encouragement to consider multiple, interacting causes of behaviour, so that they may be realistically (and not manipulatively) empowered to affect whatever requires attention in their school. And it offers the pastoral team, with its important overview of pupil behaviour, practical strategies for clarifying the problem situations and devising appropriate changes. This book incorporates a belief in the potential for positive pastoral care and makes appropriate suggestions.

This book does not offer simple remedies or recipes which would purport to apply to all schools. Rather, it suggests practical tools to help colleagues in schools to work towards their own internal solutions, through processes of eliciting important information and developing school-based discussion.

In our work with teachers we have found many of them dissatisfied with simplistic models for understanding behaviour and with over-simple notions of cause. The ideas and strategies in this book have met a receptive response from teachers we have worked with.

Why an analysis at three levels?

One of the quicker ways of confusing a discussion of discipline is to confuse the 'level' of the things being talked about. For example, when making sense of Diana's behaviour it will be helpful to consider aspects of her and her social context (as a whole individual), but not so helpful to use an explanation such as 'schools create that sort of behaviour' (a general hypothesis about schools at large). Similarly, when making sense of the patterns of behaviour of a particular year group, for example, it will be helpful to consider aspects of that year's standing and history in the school organisation, but not so helpful to invoke an explanation such as 'they're a lazy lot' (an individual level of hypothesis). We need to make clear the level of phenomenon we are talking about, and seek our explanations at that level. This will help towards finding valid explanations, and also help us see that explanations which seemed incompatible are not necessarily so when their level is clarified.

We have chosen three main levels which arise in every school: the whole-school level, the classroom level, and the individual level.

What will I find in the chapters?

1 Chapter 1 examines how school discipline is variously perceived and variously explained, especially by teachers. We introduce the perspective of this book, which lays emphasis on understanding behaviour in its context and on giving attention to in-school aspects which teachers may influence.
2 Chapter 2 looks at whole-school patterns in behaviour. Differences between schools are discussed in terms of the informal climate. Differences within schools are discussed in terms of aspects such as curriculum, teaching methods, organisation, management, support systems and overall coherence. Strategies are suggested for identifying the aspects which deserve attention in any school, and are based on a monitoring of disruptive incidents.
3 Chapter 3 considers the classroom and its distinctive features. Strategies for addressing whole-class and part-class disruption are suggested, together with a structure for understanding pupil roles. Teachers' classroom management strategies are analysed and some possible means of supporting change are discussed.
4 Chapter 4 focuses on the individual pupil and the behaviour in a range of situations. A format is suggested for gathering teachers' perspectives on a pupil, and for handling discussion meetings so that productive strategies are developed. The particular occasions when knowledge of a pupil's family is relevant are outlined and explained.
5 Chapter 5 extends the discussion of the role of the pastoral system with regard to school discipline. In the long term it is appropriate that the pastoral curriculum brings attention to behaviour in school, and activities are suggested which focus on pupils' views of rules in school and classrooms. The long-term issues for pastoral management are discussed with particular focus on redressing the distortions which are commonly found in the role of form tutor and the role of team leader. The need for development through school-based review is briefly highlighted.

In some of the chapters there are case studies from our experience, and examples to try out, and every chapter finishes with some suggestions for group discussion or investigation in your school.

We have tried not to use impenetrable language. Colleagues from outside England and Wales have commented that our drafts used language particular to that system – 'pastoral care', 'head of house', and so on. We hope this is not too much of a problem for readers elsewhere, and hope that Chapter 5 might illuminate the tutor systems which operate in British secondary schools.

Making use of this book

For reading right through, the order of chapters is deliberate. We intend to avoid too hasty a focus on individuals by examining school and classroom contexts first, and these after considering the meaning and explanation of indiscipline.

For reading each chapter we hope to have improved the accessibility of each by starting with detailed contents and an outline, and ending each with a summary.

Once you have read this book we hope you might wish to refer to it, so we have provided a comprehensive index.

Will this book change anything?

Not on its own: but we hope it supports positive influence by readers. We hope individual readers may find something of a useful new perspective which may of itself lead to change. Moreover, we hope that some readers will take the step of joining with others in their school to address the issues of indiscipline. There is generally too little team discussion of a structured sort on these themes in our schools, and we hope that the suggestions for group discussion and investigation in each chapter can be modified and used to help this process in a creative way. Further still, we hope that issues such as pupil disruption, classroom management, understanding pupils' behaviour will all be represented in your school's staff development programme and pastoral INSET.

Writing this book has given us the challenge of putting together as a related whole our ideas on the area, and we have enjoyed that challenge. While we do not generally find writing easy we have, perhaps perversely, found it enjoyable. We hope you enjoy reading it.

Chris Watkins – Patsy Wagner
London
January, 1987

1 School discipline – What do we mean?

Outline

In this chapter we aim to set out and examine some of the issues which arise from different understandings of school discipline. We believe it important to recognise from the outset that a variety of views exists, among teachers, perhaps among pupils, and among investigators of the topic, and also that this is not a new or recent state of affairs.

The main sections of this chapter are arranged to examine the common explanations for indiscipline which are found in use in schools. Some of the research evidence is brought to bear on each, and the strengths and weaknesses are assessed. Consideration is also given to issues of class, gender and ethnicity.

This leads to our perspective for the remainder of the book, a perspective which focuses on schools, on teachers' influence in schools, and on what teachers can do positively in the area of school discipline. Throughout, our perspective attaches great importance to understanding behaviour in its context.

This chapter thus examines theories in action, both in school and elsewhere, and also sets up the authors' theoretical perspective. For a first reading of this book the reader in a hurry might not suffer from reading later chapters first, but in the final judgment the adequacy and implementation of our practice is related to the adequacy of our ideas.

A definition of discipline?

We do not find it possible or indeed profitable to deliver a single definition of the phrase 'school discipline'. To do so would necessarily take away from the topic one of its more important features in school, the fact that numerous views on school discipline can be found in, around and across school staffrooms. This diversity is not something we simply wish to bemoan: to some degree we believe it could not be otherwise. And, although we feel there are shortcomings in many of the views to be heard (many of these will be examined in this chapter), we do not think it profitable to expect that progress will result from authors advocating their alternative single definition for the area. (We have a similar view towards those who seek a single definition of 'pastoral care' or indeed of 'education'. Any definition arrived at would be either partial or so general that it was about as useful as a dictionary definition.)

So the diversity of connotations attached to the term 'school discipline' is inescapably important. Indeed, as authors of this text, we sometimes feared that fixed connotations of the sort we find least useful (for example, stereotypical military ones) would be attached to the title, and our underlying message might never reach potential readers for whom the title had connotations which would encourage them to reject the book. But we could find no better title to cover the area, and finally recognised that anyone who reads the book will have suppressed their own associations enough to have read past the title!

But just because we have recognised the diversity among teachers, should we necessarily conclude that it is inescapable? Would it not be a sign of progress to get the teachers in a school to work on an agreed definition of discipline and indiscipline? Our answer is: to some degree, yes. If a school staff seem very diverse and divided in their views then some degree of increased cohesion may be important for the organisation and its clients, in which case discussions on discipline may stimulate improved communication between colleagues which could in turn lead to greater cohesion. (The success of this would ultimately depend on some other aspects of the organisation – see Chapter 2). But this does not mean that a consensus has been reached on the pupil behaviours which are/are not to be seen as breaches of discipline. This would be taking the point too far. It is unrealistic to expect a consensus of this sort, since it ignores another aspect of diversity which we are about to examine – that even for a single teacher, whether a pupil action is viewed as deviant or not depends on a range of factors including time, place, audience, and aspects of the actor. So a detailed consensus is unrealistic (even though discussions around it can sometimes have profitable spin-off), and a wide diversity can prove difficult for some organisations. Thus, our strategy aims to encourage and utilise simultaneously a broad working agreement among teachers: the practices in the remainder of this book are based on this view.

To clarify the point that the perception of a pupil act as deviant varies, some examples of such variations follow:

- *Across time* Generally in school what Steve does in the middle of the school week may be viewed differently from the same thing done at the end of the week, and a further particular variation may be introduced by the teacher who observes Steve, and her/his timetable load at the time. Also, schools sometimes have 'purges' on equipment or homework or attendance or uniform. The increase in number of 'culprits' at such a time is purely a reflection of the policy of seeking them out. Also, in historical time, our definitions of deviance vary. An 'official' example is that in 1944 there were no maladjusted pupils in England and Wales, and by 1960 there were 1,742. The category of maladjustment was, however, only introduced in 1945. (There is no equally neat explanation for the rise to 13,000 by 1975.)

- *Across place* What Mary does outside the school gates may be perceived differently from the same action inside, although some schools still have a dilemma about whether this 'should' be the case. In school Mary's singing may be viewed differently in the art room, in the music room, in the head's room. Comparing different schools, what a pupil may do in one may be completely unacceptable in another.

- *According to audience* Nigel's critical comment about one of his teachers to his tutor during a discussion of Nigel's behaviour will probably be seen differently from the same comment made while his tutor is teaching the form. When visitors or other 'public' audiences are in a school, their presence is often accompanied by an additional or accentuated set of rules for what is acceptable. Behaviour is seen differently on 'public occasions'.

- *According to features of the actor* Linda has a reputation for disrupting lessons: her behaviours may be seen and responded to differently from the way in which the same behaviour by her classmates, who do not have such a reputation, is dealt with. Again, the unexplained absence of a first-year pupil is perceived differently from that of a fifth-year pupil. Denise's direct physical aggression may be seen as more deviant than Denis's. A pupil arguing with teacher may be seen in various ways, perhaps depending on whether the pupil is a child of a lawyer or of a bricklayer. John's behaviour in the corridor is viewed as 'over boisterous', but similar behaviour from Joel with Afro-Caribbean ethnic origins is perceived differently.

- *According to who is seen as harmed* Andrew's taking a ruler from his friend in the fourth year is viewed quite differently from his taking a ruler from a first-year pupil. Ann jostles people in the crowded corridor: this is viewed as 'playful' towards her apparent friends but not towards Maria in her wheelchair.

The examples given above could doubtless be extended, but we hope the point has been made. Whether a pupil's action is seen as a 'breach of discipline' will depend on who does it, where, when, why, to whom, in front of whom, and so on. We do not conclude that such variation is 'wrong' by being unjust or unfair. Rather, we recognise that complex multi-dimensional judgments are involved in the perception of behaviour, and that no simple single definition of misbehaviour could suffice. Further, we recognise how wider considerations of history, the institution, and social structure (age, class, gender and ethnicity) may inhabit these judgments of behaviour. Perhaps 'fairness' comes about through a process of public scrutiny of such judgments, rather than from expecting uniformity in the judgments.

Also highlighted through these examples is the central role played by the person who judges a behaviour to be acceptable or otherwise. Teachers make sometimes differing judgments, depending on a key process – that of deciding on a reason and motive for the behaviour: 'Jo behaves like that because of . . .', 'Jo does that in order to . . .'. In their research, Steed, Lawrence and Young (1983) showed evidence that teachers were likely to view an incident more seriously if they perceived that it was not the first incident involving the pupil, that the pupil was acting deliberately or intentionally and perhaps with malice. On the other side of this coin we also occasionally have teacher perceptions and explanations which reduce the seriousness with which a behaviour is viewed, 'Oh, Martin can't help that – it's his family,' 'Martina doesn't mean it – she follows the others.' In all these cases we can see the important role played by teachers' explanations of pupils' behaviour and of the motives which teachers attribute to pupils. These explanations will be examined in the next section.

To conclude this section on the definition of discipline, the above considerations make it less surprising that we find apparently circular definitions effective on occasion. For example, Lawrence, Steed and Young (1977) define disruptive behaviour as 'behaviour which interferes seriously with the teaching process and/or seriously upsets the normal running of the school'. Disruptive behaviour is behaviour which disrupts. Such seemingly circular definitions have, for our present purposes, the advantage that they recognise the important role of the context in judgments of what is deviant, and do not deny in such judgments the relativity which was noted above. They do not attempt to construct a definition through listing a set of behaviours which are supposedly agreed to be disruptive. Such circular definitions appear in other related fields, for example, that of children with special educational needs. The definition given in the 1981 Act states, in essence, that children with special educational needs are those children whose educational needs cannot be met without special resources. Similarly, the Underwood Committee (1955) defined the maladjusted child as the child 'who is developing in ways that have a bad effect on himself or his fellows and cannot without help be remedied by his parents, teachers and other adults in ordinary contact with him'. (We leave unanswered the question of whether such circular definitions are the best for policy documents and the competition for resources which follows.)

The fact that detailed consensus is not achievable does not mean that teachers are being highly idiosyncratic in their judgments. For, although it is the case that different teachers may perceive different pupils to be discipline problems, deviant, disruptive or disaffected on specified occasions, the themes which recur in teachers' concerns and in disruptive incidents show a sort of working consensus. Studies such as those by Bird *et al* (1980), Lawrence *et al* (1977, 1981) demonstrate that descriptions such as 'refusal' (ie refusing to be taught, refusing to obey, refusing to work, refusing authority), talking and 'rowdy behaviour' cover the behaviour in over half the disruptive incidents. This gives an interesting reflection on classrooms and schools as we know them, and on adolescents in our society. Incidents where the behaviour is described as 'bad language', 'insolence', 'slow settling', 'lateness' and 'throwing things' bring the proportion accounted for to 90% of the incidents reported. Clearly, behaviours such as these can on some occasions and in some ways disrupt some aspects of school life and constitute much of what surfaces under the theme of school discipline. But, as we have seen, there are no doubt occasions when each of these behaviours causes no disruption, so a 'cure' which focuses on the behaviour will be irrelevant. Rather, we need to examine the conditions which throw up such incidents and examine the explanations which are available, particularly the explanations given by those centrally concerned – the teachers.

Teachers' explanations of indiscipline

Closely related to the perception of an act as deviant in some way is the attribution of some motive to the actor, and an explanation for why such events occur. Thus, when investigating indiscipline in a school, it is profitable at an early stage to examine the sorts of explanations which are available in that school, which ones are commonly used, and so on. Indeed, anyone attempting to affect processes relating to discipline will soon come face to face with these explanations, and will probably be in a better position to affect them after having examined them.

Teachers' explanations reflect a number of influences. Perhaps any individual teacher's explanation will reflect aspects of that teacher's personality, but this one dimension is not nearly adequate to give the whole picture. To some extent, teachers' explanations may reflect some of the research findings which might percolate through to daily life in school, but these findings are often distorted, held uncritically, or adopted partially. Perhaps teachers' explanations reflect the need to have an explanation in order to be able to cope and to carry on with school life but, paradoxically, in many cases teachers themselves are portrayed as powerless. Perhaps teachers' explanations reflect some wider patterns in our society, as when dimensions of class, gender and ethnicity implicitly inhabit them, and as when popular explanations from newspapers and elsewhere are echoed.

But an ever present influence on the explanation a teacher gives for any particular deviant behaviour is *the situation the teacher is in* at the time. This includes the 'frame' they're in, the situation they've just come from (especially if it was with the pupil/s concerned), the audience they're talking to, the goals they may have in mind, and so on. As we shall see, explanations can vary considerably in terms of the degree of reflectiveness they incorporate; this may be saying something important about the context in which the explanation is offered. Most of us 'blame' something simple in the heat of the moment, and recognise the wider patterns on a later occasion. And many of the 'explanations' of pupils which bounce around the staffroom with the morning coffee serve as an important release from the stress of teaching – they do not necessarily appear in front of a differing audience on another occasioin, nor do they necessarily influence those teachers' behaviour towards pupils in the following lessons.

We will examine five main sorts of explanations which appear in some literature and in our experience of schools. We give them everyday titles:

> 'They're that sort of person (it's their background, family, they've always been like it)'
> 'They're not very bright, can't cope with the work'
> 'It's just a tiny minority'
> 'It's their age'
> 'This is a difficult neighbourhood'

'They're that sort of person' Although various versions of this comment are heard, many teachers also recognise that such 'typing' of pupils explains little and is unlikely to lead to constructive action. But it may be important to note that this explanation most commonly surfaces when a teacher is attempting to explain an individual pupil rather than a group or wider pattern, and it may be that the teacher is really expressing their feeling of powerlessness in that attempt to understand.

Often the comment is heard in an extended form which brings in the 'home background' of the pupil. This view is defended on occasion by vague appeals to research. But research of the 1960s which was taken to show that school success related to positive home background generally neglected to measure school features with comparable detail. And child development research of the 1970s which was taken to show that 'maladjusted behaviour' was associated with lower socio-economic groups had generally started from an 'individual' perspective anyway and thus was likely to turn up correlations with an individual's background. Such research can only ever demonstrate a partial degree of connection across a large population of pupils, and this should not be confused with demonstrating 'cause' in an individual case. For example, a large survey by Davie *et al* (1972) measured 'maladjusted behaviour' by getting teachers to complete a standardised description format (which had never been designed for this task) on pupils. They reported that about 20% of pupils from social classes IV and V were in this way classified as exhibiting maladjusted behaviour, as opposed to about 8% of social classes I and II. But this result can in no way be taken as support for the 'home background' explanation of an *individual's* behaviour – even if s/he is classifiable as social class IV or V we have no grounds for concluding that s/he is one of the individuals in this purported 20% or in the non-maladjusted 80% and, therefore, no grounds for concluding that her/his behaviour is maladjusted (or not) because of home background.

Another version of this teacher explanation implicates some aspect of the pupil's family: 'broken homes', single parent, separation, divorce, marital disharmony and so on. Those who utilise this explanation may invoke survey evidence in an attempt to support their view, but again we must not confuse partial statistical connections with 'cause' for an individual. To do so would be to ignore the great range of ways in which families respond to and cope with such conditions. Even when a family is in an unhappy situation and itself attempts to explain a child's behaviour by reference to that major source, we need to hesitate in adopting this as the sole or main explanation. Examples which contradict the 'family background' explanations are regularly found in school, for example where two children in the same family are clearly responding in markedly different ways to their family condition.

Perhaps this explanation rests on an unstated belief that behaviour at school mirrors behaviour at home. An interesting light is thrown on this view by the finding of Graham and Rutter (1970), who showed that when teachers and parents completed similar rating scales for the same children there was comparatively little overlap between the 'disorders' perceived by both groups. So, even if teachers were identifying a similar overall percentage to that of surveys, and attributing family explanations, they may be identifying a different group of children from that identified by parents!

This finding also suggests that pupils' behaviour at school may be more to do with school than with home. But evidence which contradicts the home background explanation is often resisted, as Chessum (1980) noted:

> 'Some teachers expressed astonishment when pupils were exceptionally resistant to teacher influence despite an apparently supportive home background. They were equally surprised if model pupils were inadvertently revealed to live under adverse home circumstances. Faced with a rebellious or uncooperative pupil, teachers were often prepared to assume that there *must* be something wrong at home even if no evidence was immediately available.'

Other evidence on the relation between homes and schools would confirm the suggestion that family background explanations are rarely based on detailed factual knowledge of the pupil's family.

Our final variant of the 'they're that sort of person' explanation makes no reference to home background or family relationships as parts of the explanation, but asserts that 'they're always like that' or, further 'they've always been like that'. Perhaps this embodies an implicit appeal to outdated notions on the fixed nature of a person's behaviour, or on supposed genetic influences or early experience. However, such views are not only under serious scientific question but are also not directly applicable to the individual case.

Sometimes secondary school teachers are of the view 'they were like that in primary school too'. Although this can be the case, it is not a statement of the general picture. Behaviour at secondary school is not a simple continuation of behaviour at primary school. For example, it has been shown from the Rutter *et al* (1979) research that secondary schools with poor pupil behaviour are not simply those which receive a high proportion of pupils with a record of behaviour problems at primary school. 'There was only a weak relationship between behaviour at primary and secondary schools' (Mortimore, 1980).

These three variations of an explanation need to be seen in the context in which they are put forward, including any action which may be indicated in that context. Here it may be interesting to note that the 'that sort of person' view could imply action of a variety of sorts: if the pupil is not disturbing, then no action is quite happily justified ('they're just like that'), or, if the pupil is disturbing, then it seems justified to make a referral to whoever is supposed to deal with 'that sort of person'.

saying something about classrooms, curriculum and school.

There are many varied examples of pupils who appear to have limited school abilities, who create disruptive incidents (sometimes in a highly skilful manner). To explain the disruption in terms of their abilities leaves out some very important questions. For instance, it might lead us to ignore the question, 'Why should it be *lower* ability pupils who respond in this way?' There is no clear answer that they simply do not understand the rules and expectations. If we ask this question we may have to recognise that some non-succeeding pupils are showing a response to wider features of school. As we discuss further in Chapter 2, the low status which school often affords to the low attainer may need reconsideration, as may the curriculum offer. Further, when we look at a particular example of a teacher using such an explanation about a pupil's behaviour in their classroom, we may need to consider how that classroom is organised for a range of abilities, what teaching methods are employed, how materials are suited, and so on. These are not simple issues but they are central. Classroom organisation is especially discussed in Chapter 3.

In this way we hope that the explanation 'they're not very bright' can lead to a positive consideration of the experience of educationally unsuccessful pupils in our schools. The alternative is to accept such an explanation at its face value, which would mean taking for granted that pupils of particular abilities will be disruptive. Such an alternative is unacceptable since it also takes for granted that we cannot improve their educational experiences. The explanation: 'If they're not very bright, there's nothing we can do about it' appears to call for a passive response. In such a way some people are predicting that lack of educational success has no chance of being reversed.

'*It's just a tiny minority*' This explanation takes a wider-than-individual view, recognises that there may be a pattern in the numbers of pupils involved, but locates the cause in a very small number. This sort of explanation can be found in contexts other than schools and attempts to convince us that the source of the behaviour which threatens us is a limited one.

Some evidence from schools paints a rather different picture. When Lawrence *et al* (1977) studied the 101 disruptive incidents which teachers at an urban comprehensive school monitored during a week in November and a week in February, they found that 15% of the pupils on roll were mentioned by name in connection with one or more incidents. Hardly a tiny minority. But was there a 'hard core' within this 15%? Perhaps our attention is drawn here to the fact that pupils who were named in disruptive incidents in both weeks amounted to 1% of the roll. Are these the hard core, responsible for the serious incidents? Perhaps not, since a total of 9% of the incidents were viewed by staff as 'very serious' and numbers of these involved large groups of pupils. Overall this evidence suggests a picture of more general disruption with a varying group of pupils involved, each no doubt playing a different part in the disruptive incident.

Thus, it may be more profitable to examine the inter-relationship of a number of pupil roles (see Chapter 3) than to locate 'the' cause in one or two individuals.

Another feature of the 'it's a tiny minority' explanation is that it may contain a view that 'tiny minorities' are distinctly different from 'us': they are portrayed as obeying very different rules (or no rules) and are so different (from us) that it's unlikely we would be able to understand them. Thus, the accentuation of differences is achieved. But any real differences are often greatly exaggerated in the process. This is an important process to identify and can be powerful in its effects at both individual and social levels: it is similar to the process of scapegoating. One of the methods we have found useful for raising this issue with teachers is that of simulating a classroom, in which it soon becomes clear that many teachers can become truly engaged in enacting the deviant pupil. Disruptive pupils are not an inherently different group but the pressure to portray them that way seems strong. We are regularly surprised at the considerable hesitation on the part of experienced teachers in talking about or admitting their own disruptive behaviour on occasion in their own schooling.

The 'it's only a tiny minority' explanation is often associated with a clear implication for action – identify them and separate them, whether punitively or non-punitively. 'If we get rid of the troublemakers, everything will be all right'. But that is no solution in the long run. As Rabinowitz (1981) has pointed out, unless such separation is strictly temporary, the facility for separating pupils will tend to 'silt up'. One has only to recognise that the school may play a part in the generation of problems to see that separation to some other provision works once only: when it is full, schools continue to want to refer to the provision they have become accustomed to. 'Pressures build up within (the schools) for more provision, which is then created – and soon fills up, and so on. In this way many problems of behaviour are apparently coped with, more are created, fewer are solved.'

During the 1970s an embodiment of the sort of action which may be linked to the 'tiny minority' view was to be observed in the rapid growth of special units for disruptive, suspended, and other pupils, on-site and off-site, part-time and full-time. Both of the authors were involved at times in the management of such provision. Major difficulties exist for the aims and rationale, referral and clientele, methods and achievements of such provision. In spite of our belief that special units can be important in particular circumstances (for example, when a pupil *temporarily* needs educational support or an environment with relaxed demands), we do not see them as successful in coping with disruptive behaviour, mainly because their practice so firmly locates the cause with the pupil. Thus, it is hardly surprising that any purported achievements on this front may not transfer back to the ordinary classroom context if the pupil returns – Daines (1981) suggests that 'problem behaviour reappeared in over 60% of re-integrated pupils'. In many cases such units seem to be operating as alternative education contexts for fourth and fifth year low-attaining pupils who do not return to the 'ordinary' clasroom context.

This last point suggests that there is another pattern to be explained.

'It's their age' This explanation seems remarkably powerful as an explanation of some of the data available on the ages of pupils who disrupt. However, it can be meant in two rather differing ways.

Sometimes 'it's their age' can be put in a dismissive way, as though it were a complete explanation which required no response. On such occasions stereotypical views of adolescents as moody or unpredictable or having identity problems or being excessively influenced by their peers are used – as though these were realistic views of all adolescents or (to the extent that they are valid) as though they applied to adolescents alone, or to disaffected adolescents more than others. As a complete explanation for indiscipline in school this view cannot be any more powerful through its focus on pupils' individual stage of development than can any other of the views which locate all the cause with the pupil. The sort of action which might follow from this version of the explanation could also have a dismissive flavour to it: either the active form 'get them to grow up' or the passive 'they'll grow out of it'.

Alternatively, this explanation could draw our attention to one of the stronger and most replicated patterns in school indiscipline – its considerable increase in the fourth and fifth years of the secondary school. But it is only a shorthand form of communication which describes this pattern as a product of pupils' age: the explanation does not lie in any absolute quality of age (ie of being 15 years old) but rather in the position which the pupils have reached in their years of schooling (ie one or two years before the officially permitted leaving point). Thus, to some extent the pattern reflects pupils' increasing awareness of the impending transition to non-school life, and the lack of perceived connection of their school life to their future. Here curriculum, content, teaching approaches and teacher–pupil relations are variously brought into focus, as are organisational aspects. While school continues to be one of the most rigidly age-segregated organisations in our society, it is surprising that we do not make more creative use of this aspect in the service of engaging adolescents and their striving for recognition as young adults. We generally fail to reflect much progression in the status and responsibility which is afforded to pupils as they progress through the school organisation. As a result, many are able to exercise only minimal responsibility (sometimes only the self-restraint which teachers wish) at school, which is in marked contrast to their responsibilities at home and in part-time employment (Bird *et al* 1980).

In a slightly oblique way this increase in problem behaviour in the fourth and fifth years is also reflected and recognised by teachers in their changing explanations of deviance through the school years. First-year pupil deviance attracts explanations of emotional disturbance or poor socialisation ('they're that sort of person'). Second years are seen as boisterously testing out the school limits ('it's their age'). But by mid-fourth or fifth year pupil disaffection is more likely to be viewed as a deliberate rejection of school values and school work. These differences may have some credibility but it would be short-sighted to believe that only fourth and fifth years are showing a rational response or have a critique to articulate – it may be happening in the earlier years too, where disaffection may start but be shown in less disruptive ways.

Thus, the explanation 'it's their age' can be productive to the extent that it draws our attention to wider patterns in the school and focuses attention on curriculum and transition, rather than simply ascribing the phenomena of deviance to a fixed view of adolescence.

'This is a difficult neighbourhood' This explanation can be given a dismissive interpretation, or alternatively can lead to the consideration of another set of highly important patterns.

The first interpretation locates the cause of indiscipline in the neighbourhood in a way which is like a larger version of the 'family background' explanation discussed earlier. It often makes associations with particular characteristics of the families in the school's catchment area, but these are not always detailed or accurate. As before, this sort of explanation directs no attention to the school itself: it could be portraying school as a fixed entity of unquestionable form, to which some neighbourhoods react differently from others. This cannot be taken as the full picture, since it does not fit the facts.

All the well-known 'school differences' research in England and Wales (eg Power *et al*, 1967; Reynolds, 1977; Rutter *et al*, 1979) has shown that schools in similar or the same neighbourhoods can be associated with differing pupil behaviours (delinquency, attendance, behaviour, achievement). What we may learn from these studies is that 'neighbourhood' is no simple explanation, and that we must again bring school back into the picture (through routes outlined in the next chapter).

This explanation has within it a potential reference to another important consideration: mention of neighbourhood is sometimes an implied mention of socio-economic class and it is strongly the case that educational success through schools is distributed differently along class lines. And so to a significant degree is school indiscipline. We do not view socio-economic class as some single 'variable' or a simple set of categories, but we nevertheless feel there are important patterns to explain. We cannot ignore the issue of class because it is not neat to analyse: it is a day-to-day pressing issue as evidenced by the fact that much school indiscipline is associated with older working-class pupils.

In our effort to explain such a phenomemon, it is not adequate to resort to another version of locating cause in pupils' background, for example, by suggesting that working-class pupils have less self-control or some other supposedly important characteristic – to do so would leave school out of the picture again, and would tend to portray such deviance as uncontrolled or irrational. As has already been outlined, disaffected pupils often have a clear critique of school. As research for the Hargreaves Report showed (ILEA, 1984), fifth-year pupils had similar attitudes to school, teachers and the curriculum, whether they came from manual or non-manual home backgrounds.

On the other hand, neither is it adequate to respond to the patterns in disruption by portraying the school as an agency for reproducing a class-dominated society, part of which involves the oppression of working classes through the imposition of schooling. Such an approach can all too easily fall into the trap of romanticising the school pupils in question as working-class heroes, whose disruption is their expression of resistance to schooling. Pupils do not see it that way; teachers are not simply agents of an oppressive state; schools are not mere arms of the body of the state.

With a more complex analysis, Willis (1977) suggests that many working-class pupils have spotted the contradiction between school's espoused goal of 'opportunity for all' and the differentiating of real outcome along broadly class-associated lines. With a critique of school and perhaps some experience of failure they tend towards a 'schooling is not for me' position. Up to this point in the argument there is no explanation of why their disaffection should turn to disruption: it could equally well lead to truancy or other less disruptive withdrawal. But here it is suggested that the pupils in question are engaged in a process of creating their own culture, and that this process draws on a range of sources (largely outside school) which are salient to them and their future adult identities. Thus, the culture produced has importance for the group of older working-class male pupils, their role in school, and a wider class culture to which this is all inextricably linked – in the case of Willis's research, the shop-floor working-class culture. Parallels are suggested between such pupils' behaviour and shop-floor life, especially in the areas of relations with authority, conformity and with other cultural groups. In this portrayal the pupils' creation of their cultural style is seen as their positive response to finding no purpose in education as presented. Their disruption creates excitement and enjoyment, and their forms of deviance were chosen because they 'felt right' to their view of themselves at the same time as 'resonating' with their wider life experiences. In this account, school is not portrayed as a single entity, or as simply having one 'set of values', or as having oppressive aims: indeed, teachers spend time and energy with such pupils in a very well-meaning way on themes including careers education. But the pupil culture, which also cannot be viewed as displaying a simple 'set of values', serves to block teaching efforts and prevent the realisation of liberal educational aims.

Willis's argument is persuasive in the way it applies to a group of boys who are heading for manual labour after their experience of a predominantly working-class secondary modern school. His description perhaps resonates with many other experiences in schools, although it is not (and does not claim to be) a complete picture of schooling. Fundamental questions arise from this account about the role of school in the reproduction of society, and what school has to offer such working-class pupils. This question becomes accentuated in the sort of comprehensive school which judges its success mainly on public examinations, and these processes of disaffiliation could become stronger in all schools in an age of structural youth unemployment.

Since this explanation of school indiscipline implicates the widest patterns in our society, it may be appropriate that any response would implicate the widest features of school. Certainly the issue of how schools relate to the various cultures around them and in their midst, through more than a friendly recognition in this case that some disaffected pupils are 'street-wise', raises the issue of how the curriculum prepares for 'life as lived'. This is not a simple argument for relevance or for uncritical acceptance of shop-floor morality! It would seem clear that the imposition of formal authority by a school in an attempt to defend its contradictions could be misguided (as, at a smaller level, would be teacher denigration of pupil culture as it runs the risk of generating a double meaning of class warfare).

From this perspective, action to reduce disruption could include: an alternative stress to that on qualifications as the school's output, the public valuing of non-conventional achievements, more collective forms of working in school, an understanding that 'the neighbourhood' is not 'out there' and so on. This, of course, is not the sort of stuff which necessarily creates major change in the class structure: it would be naive to view this as a possible role for school, or to ignore the limits on school as an agent of change in a class society (albeit a liberal social democratic one). But teachers and schools can choose to exploit the degree of autonomy which does exist between processes of schooling and processes of social reproduction (without waiting for sociologists to agree on the extent of this autonomy).

But finally this perspective makes plain the view that school deviance is unlikely to be eradicated: deviance can be viewed as an inevitable and 'normal' feature of organisations and society. This is not an argument for condoning deviance for it is also a 'normal' feature of organisations and society to set up mechanisms which attempt to control deviance. But it helps to put the task of school into realistic perspective. Some views have taken this argument further. Hargreaves (1979) argued that pupils who are seen as the 'opposition' may not need to be our main focus of concern. They show healthy signs of collectivity, and for working-class males heading toward manual labour their response in school can form an effective transition to their first job: no doubt many teachers of 'disruptive pupils' have perceived the 'well-adjusted' in their midst. As long as resources for continuing education are available for them in later life, so that they do not feel 'when you've learned it's too late', the school may have to accept its unintentional role in their development. On the other hand, pupils who are 'instrumentalists' or 'indifferent' in school can be seen as a cause for concern, since their response in school is towards the individualism which increasingly characterises school and which is of greater concern from the perspective of the solidarity of society as a whole.

It is perhaps worth noting that the order in which we examined the five teacher explanations for indiscipline was in a rough way based on a developing reflectiveness. In other words, some of the later ones stimulated an examination of wider patterns in indiscipline, and led to a consideration of wider issues in schooling. This is a crucial, if sometimes complicating, process for the pastoral team. To consider and respond to the wider patterns will prove ultimately more effective than just responding to the individual crisis being presented at a given moment.

However, there are two considerations which readers may have noticed by their absence, and which may be missing from teachers' explanations for a variety of reasons. The first is that although there has been explicit consideration of boys there has been no similar consideration for girls. Are they not a discipline problem? Is their deviance invisible? Second, the cultural considerations so far have focused on class, and have not included other cultural aspects. But some black pupils, especially boys with Afro-Caribbean backgrounds, seem to be over-represented in suspensions, special units and some special schools. How can we understand this?

Considerations of gender and ethnicity

At the most fundamental level we regard considerations of gender issues to be most important with regard to educational processes. These considerations should not be reduced or trivialised to some sort of simple complaining about stereotypes – that may inadvertently over-estimate the power of stereotype and in the process ignore a major issue. The concern to consider gender issues is a concern about school achievement, for girls disproportionately under-achieve. The influence of stereotype on girls' underachievement will at times need to be examined but must not be viewed as a call to change something so that schools may change.

In some ways girls may be perceived as less of a problem by their teachers: in some ways girls may be equally disaffected as boys but express their disaffection differently: in some ways girls could be affording less importance to the whole process of education. All of these aspects may be showing signs of change at the present time, with none of them applying uniformly to all girls.

Any attempt to assess whether girls and boys are equally involved in deviance would require attention to the source of information and method of information gathering.

Davies (1979) used a self-report schedule with older pupils in a mixed comprehensive in the Midlands of England, and results indicated similar deviance levels from boys and girls overall. Yet in Lawrence, Steed and Young's (1981) study of an outer London comprehensive, staff monitored incidents in which boys and girls were involved in a ratio of about 3 : 2. If these figures were in a single school, explanations could include: that girls' deviance is better hidden than boys' (a possibility which in a few minds would invoke double blame for being deviant and then devious); that girls indulge in less challenging forms of deviance and therefore are less noticed; that girls and teachers respond in a different way from boys and teachers when deviance is challenged, so that girls' deviance is reported less. With the little research evidence available the last two explanations receive some support.

The forms of deviance which some girls are reported to engage in more than boys are, in the early years of secondary school, forms of avoidance and passivity, perhaps passing lesson-time by creating fantasies linked to pop culture, and, in the later years, by creating personal time and space around school – making ways to see friends, play a radio, using school for developing their social lives, focusing on style, boyfriends and so on. These are often less challenging and aggressive forms than those used by some boys.

Although girls' peer groups are strong in the earlier years (Meyenn, 1980) there is less evidence of coherent counter-school groups than appears with the more visible male working-class examples. Perhaps when they do occur it is in the later years of school, as in Bird's (1980) report of a group of fifth-year 'difficult' girls: 'They had become a close-knit group through a common rejection of the norms of the school. However, few of them had even been in the same tutor group or class together'. A counter-culture of similar girls is also described by Davies (1979). But perhaps there are, quite simply, fewer examples of such groups among girls.

There may be fewer examples of groups of 'difficult' girls because of other aspects of girls' lives. McRobbie and Garber (1976) suggest that there is less evidence of coherent group identities among working-class girls because of the important constraints in their lives. Thus, the particular cultures which working-class girls are creating need to be understood (and not just viewed as marginal to the males) in order to explain the apparently lower levels of girls' deviance in schools. The 'culture of the bedroom' in earlier years refers to poster, music and youth culture which is easily accommodated within the home, and the deviance in school is in the fantasy of the pop world and does not challenge school. In later years, the culture of asserting 'femaleness' relates to a focus on physical maturity, make-up and sexuality rather than on schoolwork, and with a feeling of being successful in 'the real world' of adult relationships their deviance in school does not present a position of conflict or aggression towards teachers. In this way McRobbie and Garber argue that, despite less challenging deviance from girls, we should not assume they are any less critical of their schooling.

Whichever explanation is confirmed by further evidence, teachers' responses to girls and to boys still have to be taken into account. On occasion teachers attempt to control girls verbally, whereas more physical strategies may be used with boys. Perhaps this reflects the difference in the teachers' perception of girls and boys. Davies (1984) suggests that boys were seen as more difficult to control but were more easily understood: they were seen as having a greater commitment to work and their deviance was overt. This combination of 'deviant yet committed' probably shows how higher activity levels of some boys in classrooms can influence teachers' other judgments, for example, of pupil ability. As Walden and Walkerdine (1985) have shown, teachers unintentionally differentiate their explanations of the classroom performance of pupils, seeing boys as 'bright' and girls as 'hardworking'.

Finally, although it is difficult to find clear evidence for any reason other than the power of historical and cultural stereotype, a number of teachers seem anxious about how to respond to deviance from girls. 'Problem' girls are seen as a 'bigger problem' than boys on occasion, when the deviance is of a challenging variety. And on other occasions a passive or evasive response may be tolerated more from a girl than it would be from a boy. These particular examples should be seen within the overall patterns of teacher–pupil interaction, especially in the classroom, and the way these patterns relate to gender, the higher activity levels of boys, the different interactional openings which boys and girls use toward teachers, and, perhaps most important, the subtle, unintended difference in teachers' perceptions of each gender and their abilities – all of these require our attention in the attempt to develop greater gender equity in schools.

The final aspect to consider in teachers' explanations of indiscipline is that of ethnicity. We do not use the term race since it supports a notion that what we are considering had biological origins, whereas in fact we need to consider a social phenomenon in society. Despite the potential strength of the cosmopolitan nature of Western Europe, minority ethnic groups are still faced with discrimination on a range of fronts. In this context black pupils are creating their adult identities in ways which aim to preserve self-respect but on occasion these ways seem to generate problems with teachers, who may then come to view those pupils as problems.

In this section on ethnicity, research and views about black Afro-Caribbean pupils in school are quoted, in order to raise some issues at the *general* level about school and culture, in the hope that the general interpretation of pupil behaviour can be widened. This is a very different task from focusing on an individual pupil of Afro-Caribbean or any other cultural background. On such occasions the generalisations are of no help, and this section should not therefore be read as if it were possible to conclude: 'Oh, Afro-Caribbean lads are like that.' Probably there is only one generalisation which is worth keeping in mind about such pupils – that they are most likely to have suffered racist injustice in our society.

Boys with Afro-Caribbean cultural origins can become the focus of teachers' attention. For some, their route to a male adult identity is centrally concerned with the achievement of 'style', generating a visible social reputation which is expressed through dress, music, forms of talk, relation to girlfriends, and relation to school. School itself takes on an importance as a forum for social interaction with friends and it is this aspect which may bring conflict with teachers if it appears to clash with the teacher's view of things. Certainly such aspects as continual dialogue with friends and an apparent focus on friends to the detriment of work will not be received kindly by many teachers. But the description so far should not be seen as supporting a single stereotype, especially one about commitment or lack of commitment to school achievement. It would be wrong to conclude that the pupils did not value education, as Furlong (1984) has shown. The pupils he studied were committed to education, felt it had relevance to future careers, and were keen to achieve in these terms: they valued jobs which carried entrance qualifications, and their families emphasised school achievement. *But* it did not follow that these pupils would therefore conform to the school expectations on behaviour – a reputation for style could not be achieved that way. This position, which might seem contradictory to some outside observers including teachers, was especially highlighted by a group of boys who were seen as difficult yet almost never truanted. Their allegiance to school success was strong, and in this way they differ markedly from the working-class white boys described by Willis.

Girls with Afro-Caribbean aspects to their culture may provide a similar picture in some respects. If we take seriously the culture these young people are producing and how it relates to their view of adult life the picture may again make sense. Fuller's (1982) account suggested that the black girls she studied appeared disaffected; they irritated teachers, who perceived them as problems, yet were committed to school. Although they were seldom engaged in overt conflict, their deviance was not a sign that they viewed school as irrelevant. They put a value on school's role in gaining qualifications for jobs, but this in no way implied conformity. For these girls their need to work in the future, even if married, was placed alongside their desire to create the impression they felt most appropriate in the eyes of boys, particularly not to be seen as soft.

None of these 'findings' should be over-generalised: this could inadvertently support stereotyping. Their importance lies in directing our attention to a range of issues in understanding the culture which young people are creating, and thus illuminating the patterns which may exist in behaviour. Young people's views of adult identity and its creation are centrally important, and are not easily influenced by school. It would be a mistake, therefore, for school to ignore the culture young people create and, in a society as diverse as ours, attempt to superimpose its own. A wider set of perceptions is required in a multicultural society.

One theme which has recurred in the preceding brief considerations of class, gender and ethnicity is how school deviance may or may not demonstrate a rejection of one of the supposed purposes of school: the gaining of qualifications for entry into those jobs which require them. No simple connection is demonstrated, and therefore a sceptical stance is needed toward teacher explanations of the type 'S/he's messing about becaue s/he doesn't see the point of school'. Further, it is important to note how rapidly young people's opportunities on leaving school have changed since 1980 (and therefore since some of the studies quoted above). *Twelve million* young adults are unemployed in Western Europe in 1987. In some parts of Britain it is the minority of school leavers who find a job. Will this economic situation affect school indiscipline? As it becomes increasingly clear that school's credentialist function is questionable for many more pupils, it is possible to argue that more pupils will adopt the position of 'school is not for me' and perhaps express this in disruptive ways (unless schools change). Little clear evidence is yet available, but Coffield's (1986) research in the North East of England, where industry has collapsed and extended deprivation is developing, may be relevant. Among long-term unemployed young people the view that 'if you work hard you'll get on' is still supported, and school does not become a target of blame by implication in their lack of opportunity. While this may allow some schools to breathe a sigh of relief for their discipline problems, the personal and social cost which follows from these young people *blaming themselves* is not a proud achievement for anyone.

Nevertheless, despite such urgent challenges, this evidence can be viewed as supporting, for the moment at least, the main argument which has been developed in this book – that the patterns of indiscipline inside a school should mainly be understood by reference to features inside the school. Before giving a more developed statement, it is perhaps worth pausing to check whether the argument so far can be supported by evidence from teachers at large, and whether the seeds of a more positive strategy can be identified.

A survey of teachers' explanations of disruption

In the spring of 1981 a visiting American (Dierenfield, 1982) surveyed teachers in a 10% sample of mixed comprehensive schools in England. With a high response rate for postal questionnaires (over 50%) the views of a number of teachers in each school were obtained.

In response to a question which invited teachers to rate ten provided 'causes' of disruptive behaviour in comprehensive schools, the proportion who rated each item as 'an important cause' was:

Unsettled home environment	49.6%
Peer pressure	35.6%
Lack of interest in subject	30.7%
General disinterest in school	30.5%
Pupil psychological or emotional instability	29.4%
Inability to do classwork	21.9%
Revolt against adult authority	20.8%
Lack of self-esteem	13.7%
Dislike of teacher	12.7%
Use of drugs	4.9%

Here a number of the 'explanations' we have discussed so far receive support. There also seems to be support for the idea of locating some of the 'cause' in school processes (although it is always possible to endorse 'lack of interest in subject' as a statement about the pupil rather than the subject). A range of items is endorsed, and each item receives a range of ratings, reflecting the variation in explanations. Interestingly, head-teachers and their deputies endorsed home, peers, and instability as important causes more than the teachers.

When attention turns from 'causes' to responses there are interesting changes in the picture. Of twenty-two possible 'factors' for controlling disruptive behaviour, the ten most frequently rated as very important were:

Positive teacher personality	89.7%
Effective teaching methods	87.6%
Establishing and maintaining behaviour standards early on	86.3%

Firm support of teacher discipline measures by head	70.8%
Consistent application of behaviour standards to all pupils	69.3%
Support of school by parents	68.7%
Treating causes of behaviour problems	66.6%
Influence of head	56.0%
Pastoral care programme	40.3%
Strict disciplinary measures by teacher	39.9%

Here the teacher and aspects of the school are strongly in the picture, and the overall figures for endorsement of control factors are much higher than those for causes. Perhaps this reflects the practical and pragmatic approach of teachers. Factors such as expulsion/suspension, special classes, streaming, corporal punishment, and school social worker received less (but perhaps still significant) support. Heads and deputies were found to endorse more strongly than average those factors which engaged parents and the pastoral care programme (55% of heads and deputies rated the latter as very important – the same endorsement as they gave to the item 'influence of head').

To close this examination of teachers' explanations it remains to review the aim of this section. It has not been to mount an attack on explanations which are commonly used in school: such criticism rarely promotes change. Rather the aim has been to evaluate the various aspects which are drawn to our attention. Nor has the intention been to equip the reader with information to knock down partial explanations in the staffroom: that is an energy-sapping process which is unlikely to lead to change since it forgets the expressive function of staffroom communication. Rather, the aim has been to demonstrate that some explanations are more reflective than others in that they incorporate consideration of wider patterns. Thus, it will follow that the practical strategies advocated in this book will seek to create occasions (not in the staffroom) where colleagues may together reflect on the patterns in their own school. If such occasions are supported by well structured information, we find that the differences in teachers' general explanations can be managed without conflict. Finally, the intention has not been to portray teachers' explanations either as personal idiosyncrasies or as fixed: as Steed (1983) has observed, in another country's education system with more flexible organisational arrangements and resources, responses to difficult pupils can be different: 'The first question many Danish teachers ask themselves about the pupil who is difficult is "What have I done or failed to do that could account for this?" The term generally applied to such children's behaviour is "tiredness of schooling".'

Finally, a short consideration of pupils' explanations of disruption is worthwhile: it is short because this book is about teachers working with other teachers on what they can jointly resolve (and so we hope to avoid the charge which is rightly made of many books on schooling – that the consideration of teachers' perspective outweighs that of pupils). Since disruption is mainly defined by the teacher it might be expected that pupils do not have an elaborate view of causes as located in pupils. Indeed, there are some suggestions that pupils give general explanations for classroom disruption by reference to the major feature in their eyes – the teacher. Pupils identify specific 'offences' committed by teachers, which are, from the pupils' point of view, the precipitating causes of disruption. Examples include showing 'contempt' through being distant, or 'anonymity' through not knowing pupils names (Marsh *et al*, 1978). This bears some similarity with the illuminative work of Tattum (1982), who showed that pupils in special units utilised the following explanations:

1 It was the teachers' fault
2 Being treated with disrespect
3 Inconsistency of rule application
4 We were only messing – having a laugh
5 It's the fault of the school system

While the content of these explanations is taken seriously, it is also clear that they function as a form of justification, or what might be termed 'excuses'. Rather than risk dismissing them, it is important to note that these explanations are potentially effective attempts to neutralise the deviant identity which is being cast upon the person. In the terms of Sykes and Matza (1957) these are examples of:

> Denial of responsibility   (1)
> Denial of injury   (4)
> Denial of the victim
> Condemning the condemners (2)
> Appeal to higher loyalties   (3,5)

all of which are regularly evidenced in school. The important point here is to recognise that, rather than dismiss these as excuses, we should see them as responses which self-respecting adolescents would be likely to adopt in the face of accusation.

Finally, many teachers who have discussed with pupils the reasons

Here social workers, education welfare officers, educational psychologists or child psychotherapists (some of each of whom do seem to be practising with a highly individualistic view of people) are perhaps engaged (and in this process their ability to 'fix' certain individual problems is mistakenly overestimated, sowing the seeds for teachers' subsequent disappointment at their offering).

These courses of action all direct attention away from the teacher or teaching towards the pupil, background, history, and non-teaching professionals. It is a little too simple to suggest that the point of the explanation is to 'let teacher off the hook' since this itself simplifies a multiple causality, and, indeed, many teachers will invest long hours of individual work with the pupils so described. Nevertheless, the lack of reference to teacher or teaching is noteworthy since it might be implied that the state of affairs being explained is not amenable to change by experimenting with the teacher or teaching approach. As a temporary expression of how powerless we feel in some situations, this is understandable, but it does not serve us well as a more long-standing view since it fuels and maintains that feeling of powerlessness. In a similar way this explanation also leaves the pupil out of the picture and embodies a deterministic style of prediction about their behaviour. The pupil is not portrayed as having a view on their own choice of behaviour, and therefore is not to be seen as a potential agent for change in that behaviour, again disempowering another major person in the event.

But perhaps the most serious fault in such 'explanations' is that they do not recognise or make use of the significant and informative variation which occurs in all social behaviour. As we show in Chapter 4, an approach which takes this into account, 'the whole-individual perspective', can lead to a variety of strategies for action following a structured reflection on such patterns.

To continue, we find that some teacher explanations *do* show evidence of reflecting on patterns of behaviour.

'They're not very bright, can't cope with the work' This teacher explanation could at first sight seem like a variant of the previous one. We could point out that it seems deterministic, perhaps is based on little clear information about the pupil's strengths and weaknesses, appeals to outdated notions of ability as fixed, doesn't recognise the varied nature of people's abilities, and so on. But to carry on in this vein would ignore the fact that judgments about pupil ability have an extra significance in the school context and are closely connected with the way school is organised. Therefore, this explanation of deviance is also

for school disruption, will have encountered the view, which is akin to that underlying this book, that deviance varies across contexts in a most important way. 'It varies between lessons and who the teacher is . . . you act up to them in their own way.' (Quoted in Bird *et al*, 1980).

The perspective of this book

Given the examination in this chapter of the range of influences on school indiscipline, it is clear that behaviour which disrupts school can have:

- personal aspects, relating to the pupil(s) and their lives
- institutional aspects, relating to teachers, classes, organisation, and so on
- cultural aspects relating to wider aspects of class, ethnicity, and gender.

In even a single example of pupil behaviour we can sometimes recognise all three aspects. This recognition forms the overall perspective which acts as a backdrop to all other considerations. To omit any of these aspects from our overall understanding is to adopt a partial view.

Focusing now on the more particular consideration of what a school can *do* about the indiscipline it experiences, it is clear that the second of the aspects listed above is open to modification by the school. A range of evidence suggests that schools can influence the patterns in their midst by adapting their own processes. In contrast, the personal dispositions of pupils and the structural features of our society are hardly open to short-term influence by school, and even in the long term it is common to exaggerate the effects of school on such aspects. This, however, should not be taken as a statement that their consideration may be dropped. In individual circumstances the school will rightly consider aspects of pupils' home life, especially family crises. And in the wider pattern of pupil behaviour the school should be considering whether cultural processes are being reflected. But it would be defensive and short-sighted to attempt an explanation of school indiscipline by resource only to the personal and cultural: the institutional requires extra attention. The argument being put forward here is close to that which distinguished between 'predisposing conditions' and 'precipitating factors' of behaviour. We may regard a whole range of societal issues as predisposing and long-term influences on school discipline (as long as we also remember that they may be achieving influence only because of the way school is presently constructed). With this as context we can then turn to the precipitating factors which are to be found within the school. This is not a message of blame, but an empowering message that says teachers can make a difference. In this way, with a reduction in precipitating factors, indiscipline may be reduced but not eliminated.

As a book which is about school and for teachers in their relations with pupils, this text focuses on what teachers can do differently. This does not mean a list of generalised prescriptions, suggestions, or recipes. Rather, some approaches are elaborated which serve to generate useful data on patterns of disruption, initiate structured discussions on the possible influences, and lead forward to experiment. These approaches all work towards generating increased communication between teachers on these themes – a positive side effect is therefore the reduced isolation of individual teachers (especially on such stress-inducing issues as clasroom discipline) and the enhanced levels of communication in the school at large. For pupils at large the main effect is that of being able to work in an atmosphere where self-direction is more likely and the chances of getting what may be wanted from school are enhanced, while for those particular pupils on whom the disciplinary eye regularly rests the chances of avoiding a damaging career through school are increased. Thus we regard school indiscipline as:

a informative,

b to some degree inescapable, and

c to some degree potentially damaging (for teachers and pupils)

And our perspective adopts an approach which

a aims to ensure we learn from the evidence,

b reduces to some degree the overall level, and

c minimises damage for those involved.

In such an approach there will be elements of re-examining the existing explanations and of regarding pupil behaviour as conscious choices which need to be understood in relation to a variety of influences.

Thus, the overall perspective on indisciplined behaviour, outlined in more detail in the next three chapters, is one which views behaviour as a complex interrelation of numerous elements, the most fruitful for teachers being the most immediate ones of the social context – the school.

Finally, it seems appropriate to indicate that this perspective does not lead to some of the responses which are often talked about in discussions of discipline. We will mention three, and hope to inoculate against disappointment any reader who is expecting further discussion on these.

First, 'early detection'. This view argues that schools should identify pupils who are likely to cause disruption and apply preventive measures early. As in other areas, this strategy does not seem successful (Wedell and Lindsay, 1980). Perhaps it locates too much cause in the pupil whose identification is sought, rather than in the context in which disruptive behaviour arises. Early identification at primary school is particularly dubious, given the weak relationship between behaviour at primary and secondary schools (p 14), yet in some areas views on pupil misbehaviour are still passed from primary to secondary in such a way that the main effect could be that reputations are cemented (this point does not apply to well-structured information on other behaviour and learning styles).

Second, referral systems. For the general perspective of this book, the use of referral systems (both internal to the school and external to welfare network agencies) will not be considered in depth. We have mentioned special units (p 17) and the attendant difficulties in their operation. But, in general, referral systems can operate to focus the main discussion of discipline on to individual pupils rather than on to the context. Further, we are aware that many teachers are nowadays wary even of internal referral systems if they are operated without considerable thought – the experience of precipitating a pupil into a referral funnel by mentioning her/him to head of year, only to find that one has no further contact until the head has taken action, is what can make teachers feel that referral systems escalate matters rather than solve them.

Third, punishment. This strategy will not be discussed in depth for a number of reasons. For over fifty years studies have demonstrated that praise is a much more powerful influence on behaviour than is punishment. Punishment serves mainly to repress particular behaviour rather than to educate into new ones. Commonly, the process of punishment in schools is carried out with little reference to an understanding of the social context in which the disruptive behaviour took place. And evidence from whole-school studies such as the Rutter research questions the usefulness of punishment:

'punishments were not related to behaviour, except for extreme levels of corporal punishment (both official and unofficial), which was associated with misbehaviour. The punishment policy perhaps reflected the history and traditions of school rather than the actions of the pupils.' (Mortimore, 1980)

But in another way Mortimore's last comment perhaps raises the main occasion when punishment may be important in schools: when a clear and important value of school and society is embodied in a rule which seems important for educational ends. An example might be that of disallowing racist name-calling. With such examples Durkheim's rationale for punishment, 'to affirm, in the face of an offence, the rule that the offence would deny' (quoted in Hargreaves, 1979), would seem to be relevant. However, to attempt the justification of numerous rules and associated punishment by recourse to this rationale would be ineffective, since the school would be risking the possibility of becoming counter-productive and alienating.

Summary

Chapter 1 has argued that numerous definitions of indiscipline may exist, and that indiscipline cannot be defined without reference to the context of behaviour. Teachers' explanations have been examined and their various strengths and weaknesses assessed. The common trend of explaining disruption by recourse to features inside the pupil and outside the school has been noted.

The overall perspective of this book is that behaviour which is seen as deviant in school can have personal, institutional and cultural dimensions. A practical strategy for teachers to understand and minimise indiscipline starts by focusing on the institutional with an awareness of the personal and cultural. Subsequent chapters promote this strategy at whole-school, classroom and individual levels via methods for gathering important information for group discussion by teachers.

Suggestions for discussion/investigation

1 Listen to conversations in your school (not at coffee break!) when discipline is being discussed and identify the sorts of explanations which are implicitly being used. Which are commonly used? To what purposes? Compare with pp 12–19.
2 Collect examples of how the same behaviour may/may not be seen as deviant depending on context and other features (pp 8–9). Share your observations with one or two colleagues.
3 Conduct an informal survey amongst the staff on their view about causes of disruptive behaviour, using Dierenfield's format (p 28). Compare your school's responses with the general picture in 1981, and find an appropriate channel for feeding your results back to your colleagues.

2 The whole-school perspective

Outline

This chapter focuses on the whole-school level of understanding discipline and indiscipline. This is a focus which may typically receive little attention. Yet without this level of analysis, much of teachers' other efforts may be going to waste.

The chapter starts with a recognition that different schools are associated with different patterns in numerous pupil behaviours. These differences between schools are understood in terms of important informal features of schools: climate, interpersonal issues and so on (rather than the formal or more tangible features). This leads to a consideration of polarising and rigid climates.

Within any one school a further set of patterns in pupil behaviour will be found. These differences can be associated with a wide range of features. Four main areas are discussed: curriculum and teaching methods, organisational aspects, staff aspects, and wider aspects to the school system.

Strategies for identifying the aspects which deserve attention in any particular school are presented. Methods for monitoring behaviour are suggested, as they generate potentially powerful information for improvement. Some of the issues in handling the information which is generated, and the generating of creative discussions are anticipated.

Schools make a difference

Research findings now well substantiate the view which many teachers and parents have always held – that different schools have different overall effects on a variety of outcomes for their pupil groups.

Power *et al* (1967) showed that schools with comparable intakes in the same area were associated with markedly different rates of delinquency among their pupils. Cannan's (1970) data suggested that even the style of delinquency and its age of onset varied across comparable schools: one was associated with more petty theft while in another pupils specialised in 'taking and driving away'. On a different measure, studies such as that by Galloway *et al* (1982) demonstrate large and consistent differences between secondary schools in the number of pupils excluded or suspended on disciplinary grounds. Studies by Reynolds and Murgatroyd (1977) and others have shown that levels of truancy differ consistently across schools with similar intakes in the same area, and that these differences maintain over some years. Another pupil outcome, that of success in public examinations, has been shown by a number of studies, for example, Chapman (1979), Steedman (1980), ILEA (1982) to be affected by schools and type of schools. One of the better known studies in recent years is that of Rutter and his team (1979), who showed significant differences between twelve London schools on a range of behaviours.

Findings such as the ones outlined serve to demonstrate that schools do make a difference. This contrasts with the more pessimistic view prevalent in the 1970s that schools were unlikely to have major effects in the face of home background and social class (a view supposedly based on sociological studies of the time which actually measured nothing of the school process). But the search for school differences *in contrast* to home differences is a fruitless one since it may over-simplify a complex situation. The effects of development on young people are hardly likely to be attributable to home *or* school, one or the other. It is more likely that both can be powerful influences, and ideally both act as positive influences in an additive way. This then paints a more complex picture, with positive school effects having to work in consort with positive family/home effects. Similarly, although it is likely that school is not a sufficiently powerful social agency to compensate fully for larger aspects in society such as social disadvantage, it does seem to be the case that a school can to a greater or lesser degree prevent social disadvantage becoming educational disadvantage as well. So, when the influences outside school are negative for a young person's development, school can to some degree protect the pupil from the effects of such predisposing conditions.

However, if schools do make a difference, it is not yet completely clear *how* the differences are generated. What is it about a school which has an effect on pupils? And what is it about pupils which is affected by schools? Is the answer the same for all pupils? These questions have not yet been fully answered by research, but for the practitioner concerned to make school effective they stimulate enquiry and clarification of how we understand the effects of school.

Understanding the whole-school effect

Present indications are that differences between schools are likely to be explained by reference to some of the less tangible features of the organisation, particularly those which describe the quality of the interpersonal relationships. Some people find this a difficult message to swallow, often because they have their own favourite theory on what makes the difference between schools, and their explanation often focuses on one simple but visible feature (size of school, age of buildings, existence of uniform for pupils, etc). But the message is a positive if complex one, since it then follows that it is within the influence of the staff of a school to make its institutional effects positive ones. But this message also confirms the point we made in the introduction – that our explanations of discipline phenomena must be at the appropriate 'level', ie if we're looking at whole-school patterns our explanations must refer to some feature of the whole school (as opposed to features of particular pupils, etc). So how then shall we describe these interpersonal qualities of our organisation?

The notion of 'school climate' has been researched since 1960 and has been a central notion in attempts to measure the particular 'feel' or atmosphere of a school. Early studies chose to measure the leadership style and teacher/head-teacher relations, this choice having been made to parallel studies of management in industrial organisations. But later work recognised the differences between schools and industrial organisations, and thus recognised the salience of the pupil's role and perceptions. As a result, studies incorporated the pupil view and were able to show, for example, that student participation in decision-making has a significant effect on student attitudes to school (Epstein, 1981).

Additional attention has focused on school climate since the publication of the research by Rutter and colleagues (1979) which examined differences across twelve London secondary schools. The significant differences they found were explained by the different 'ethos' of schools, again pointing to the informal social relations of the school, and the informal messages which are conveyed by the organisation.

With our attention on these informal aspects of school it is not yet the case that researchers can offer us an agreed way of assessing school climate. Some regard it as a slippery notion. Indeed it is easy to question the idea of a single climate to a school: perhaps there can be differing sub-climates as is sometimes remarked about the varying 'feel' associated with different years or houses in a school.

Whether school climate is or is not easily measured does not divert us from the fact that it is connected with the school's performance on many dimensions. And it probably reflects the important yet seldom analysed *culture* of the school. This highlights the underlying assumptions about what sort of organisation the school is. In Handy's (1984) terms, a school may be:

a like a club, with a web of control based on intimacy, much time spent on admitting the 'right' person;

b like a bureaucracy with organisation charts, role titles, a wealth of procedures and routines;

c like a network of teams which are grouped and regrouped to tackle various plans and problems;

d a place where the individual and her/his talents are put first and the organisation is seen as a resource.

Perhaps it is the case that rather too many secondary schools operate in the bureaucratic style without having assessed alternatives. This 'role culture' is characterised by an extended amount of formal management. There are, however, two major problems in this style and in this view of the secondary school at large. The first is that such an organisation thrives when it is doing a routine, stable and unchanging task. But surely this is not a characteristic of schools in the 1980s, with changing patterns of teaching, certification, employment and so on. The organisation with a 'role culture' finds it hard to cope with such change. The second problem with this view is that it focuses almost entirely on the formal aspects of the organisation – 'the way it's supposed to be'. This presents a problem since the formal aspects of any organisation cannot really explain all there is to that organisation: it omits all of the ways through which the formal aspects are mediated, modified, reacted to, and often ignored by the informal day-to-day practice. We need only remember examples of schools which run effectively with an absent or ineffectual head to remember that the informal system of power, communication and influence is more salient than the role titles.

When we consider processes of discipline in a school, the tendency to talk in formal terms about the organisation can be distinctly counter-productive. The tendency to call for routines to cope with situations can be an ineffective attempt at a short cut in problem-solving. Calls for absolute consistency across staff or for agreed procedures which specify teacher responses to defined pupil behaviours can be unrealistic: they ignore the complexity in teachers' decisions about deviance, seem to wish for a simpler world than we have in school and, even if agreed, are unlikely to be implemented by a large proportion of teachers. Thus, to pin too much hope on the formal aspects of our organisation is a false hope: the informal needs to maintain a high profile in our thinking.

Patterns of discipline between schools: the implications of climate

The trends which seem to be developing, judging from the results of the few studies available on discipline and school climate, confirm the importance of examining informal processes. Two linked themes emerge: that of the school with a 'polarising' ethos, and that of the school with an inflexible ethos.

A polarising climate in a school is at its most extreme when the organisation and its social messages facilitate the success of a minority through the failure of others. One element could be rigid streaming where, as early studies such as Hargreaves's (1967) showed, lower streams come to be associated with lower expectations, distinctive self-images, and a 'delinquescent' sub-culture. Lacey's (1970) study of a grammar school also suggested that processes of differentiation carried out by teachers in the normal course of their duties can unwittingly lead to polarisation in the pupil group, where the normative academic culture is also accompanied by an alternative pupil culture. More recently Woods (1979) and Ball (1981) have underlined such findings in schools since 'comprehensivisation'. Ball argues that polarisation is happening through more complex mechanisms than streams, primarily through options and curriculum choices. 'Options had apparently inherited the function of finely differentiating pupils beyond the coarse labelling of band.'

It is unlikely that schools will ever completely give up their differentiating of pupils in a society such as ours: what is at stake here is the *degree* to which polarisation occurs. By accentuating differences the school sends devaluing messages to a significant proportion of the school population, who then respond accordingly. These processes are amenable to influence and change by teachers, since they include (amongst others) the very processes which teachers create – in allocating both positive and negative reputations to various of the pupils. In schools where this is done to excess, the risk is run of generating increased levels of indiscipline from identifiable sections of the population.

By implication, part of the whole-school level of analysis should include reflecting on the school as an informal social system and trying to identify any aspects which communicate to pupils a polarising message and an accompanying difference in value. 'You're either academic or practical', the differential allocation of resources and space, the implicit 'streaming' of teachers – all these are examples of how the message can be conveyed that a particular form of success for a minority of pupils is given status, while the remainder of pupils are afforded neither success nor status. When trying to reduce the whole-school levels of indiscipline these aspects require review. In their stead we would aim to embody more valuing messages. Instead of the underlying belief that life is a zero-sum game, ie one person's gains are another's losses, we aim to show that the school has on offer signficant development for all. This does not mean ignoring pupil differences: it means respecting differences which are real, and working to implement more fully the principle of equal value.

The second aspect of school climate which has been linked to school levels of indiscipline is the theme of inflexibility. This draws our attention to a feature of teacher–pupil relations which highlights the application of rules and Reynolds' (1977) notion of a 'truce'. Having studied nine South Wales schools and their patterns of truancy, Reynolds concluded that consistent and ongoing differences between the schools could best be explained by noting that in some schools pupils and teachers struck a truce over the application of some rules, whereas in other schools pupils and teachers refused a truce. Thus, in a working-class community where some writings could lead one to expect a high degree of conflict between teachers and pupils, there was a remarkable lack of conflict in the social life and inter-personal relations in some of the schools.

'A crucial factor in determining a favourable overall response by the pupils to most of their schools lies in the degree to which both staff and pupils have reached an unofficial series of arrangements, or truces, which lay down the boundaries beyond which the participants in the schools will not carry their conflict.' (Reynolds, 1977).

Thus truces may be struck over a range of issues which are not directly related to teaching, for example, some aspects of dress, chewing gum, smoking at break, and behaviour outside school gates or school hours. Then 'lessons are no longer the focus of conflict between teacher and taught.' In the schools where no truce existed an anti-school subculture had developed by the beginning of the third year. Teachers attempted to ensure their control through increased coercion, extending to those areas of pupils' lives where they valued autonomy; pupils' commitment to school reduced, and teachers consequently had lower expectations of the pupils.

There are a number of useful implications for the pastoral team. The phenomenon which is being described in the school which refuses a truce is akin to an organisational version of escalation, similar to that which we shall consider later at the classroom level. The results suggest that it is counter-productive for a school to be involved in rigid enforcement of some rules, since this can encourage the whole system to distort into a 'discipline fixation' akin to the pastoral system at its worst. (Readers will have noted the significant exception to this point, which was discussed at the end of the last chapter, p 34). Thus, at this whole-school level the pastoral team will be needing to support an atmosphere of realism and flexibility in the school's climate for rule enforcement. To bring these issues to debate, a 'rule review' could be instituted, part of which is to ask pupils which rules they consider to have counter-productive effects.

It is not suggested that the pastoral team work towards the abolition of rules – this would be unrealistic and contrary to the view outlined in the previous chapter. But the pastoral team should be supporting a rule system which is not excessive, is meaningful to pupils, and is negotiated in the knowledge of pupils' views. A review of rules is an important task for any school, ideally at regular intervals. It is unlikely that any school is operating with the minimum effective set of rules, and we are not swayed by those who wish to label today's schools as permissive. Support for this assessment may be found in the recent review by Her Majesty's Inspectorate of 11–16 and 12–16 schools: 'None of the schools has an over-permissive regime.' (HMI, 1984).

It is important to make clear the rationale behind this approach to a flexible rule-climate. It is not the avoidance of enforcing a realistic rule because a particular pupil is perceived as 'difficult' and the teacher predicts that enforcement would create difficulty. Rather, it is the conviction that the pastoral team can happily support a rule-climate which has been effectively reviewed for its positive benefit to the main aim of the school: the pupils' education and personal development.

Having examined some of the findings on differences between schools, we now move to consider differences within schools which are often very clear to the school practitioner.

Patterns of discipline within schools

For practitioners in a particular school the notions of informal climate and its relation to discipline in different schools can prove crucial in the long term. Alongside this, in a debate amongst the staff of any one school the differences in pupil behaviour which can be observed within that organisation are likely to provide immediate and telling examples. So we now turn to consider patterns within a school, remembering that our level of analysis is still the whole school. We are not yet examining the dynamics of particular classrooms; are aiming to identify internal features of the school which are associated with differing levels of disruption.

Everyday talk in schools often makes reference to patterns within the school: 'Those second years are appalling', 'My O-level group are lovely as usual', 'Oh no – they've just come from maths'. But the powerful information embedded in the patterns is often not used, and teachers continue to feel powerless and resigned to such phenomena. Alternatively, if the initiative is taken to examine patterns of behaviour, the discussion can often lead to such supposed influences as time of the day, point in the term, and size of the school. We do not intend to deny that some such issues can influence patterns of behaviour (although evidence on the size of school issue is not consistent), but it is interesting to note that these influences often have a common feature – they are not under the direct control of teachers. This may be an example of the wider phenomenon in which teachers locate the cause for disruptive behaviour in sources other than themselves, while locating with themselves the important source of controlling disruptive behaviour (Dierenfield, 1982). Although this is perhaps defensive, it is an understandable enough feature of everyday life, where we tend to take credit for our successes and attribute the causes of our failures elsewhere. For the purposes of analysing patterns of disruption in school, however, this process does not serve us well since it can result in attention not focusing on those aspects which teachers control more directly and which have significant effects on pupil behaviour. From these considerations it follows that discussion of the school's indiscipline patterns will not develop well if it is conducted in an atmosphere which calls out defences and reactions (as it might if it were loaded with connotations of judging teachers' success and failure). But such a discussion can be conducted in a way which is very empowering to the teachers in a school.

The aspects of a school which may generate or influence patterns of disruptive behaviour by pupils are many. Almost any aspect of the organisation which carries a social message of devaluation or which generates a social effect of frustration can lead to patterns of behaviour which are not simply attributable to the particular individuals who show such behaviour. Most of the aspects which are associated with pupil indiscipline are also aspects of the organisation which centrally affect the quality of teachers' job satisfaction and teacher–pupil relations.

In an attempt to describe some of the relevant aspects of school, we use the following four headings:

Features of the curriculum, including pedagogy
Features of the school organisation and management
Features of the staff
Features of the school as a social system

Obviously these headings interrelate and all contribute to the overall climate of interpersonal relations in the school.

Features of curriculum and pedagogy

A contributory element to the low credibility afforded to pastoral care in some quarters is that it rarely stimulates discussion about curriculum issues. But the pastoral team, who are in the position of having an overview of pupils' responses to school, are in a very strong position to inform the debate about a school's curriculum. And the occasions when our attention is on patterns of discipline are no exception: the pastoral team has much important information at its fingertips. As Handy (1984) points out:

> 'one could argue that the pastoral organisation that grew up in comprehensive schools [is] an internal agency to make sure that each child got the best mix available out of the product range on offer . . . That part of the organisation ought to be the driving force in the organisation, the one that sets the priorities and the tone and calls the tunes'.

The curriculum offer in many of our secondary schools suffers from being perceived as a collection of subjects (still very similar to that of the grammar school), and this is maintained in many cases by teachers who feel most secure in their subject-teaching identities. Consequently, the climate for curricular change is often unfavourable, and what is offered to young people continues *not* to be characterised by flexibility and applicability. Yet these two qualities may be crucial in engaging the energies of a range of adolescents and thus minimising the degree of disruptiveness.

The alternative for the pastoral team is to consider the curriculum as the total learning offer provided by the school and to examine its biases, strengths and weaknesses, and the degree to which important themes and processes permeate the whole. From this perspective it may not be surprising to find such phenomena as: a narrower offering for those pupils perceived as of average and below-average ability; a variety of unbalanced offerings (eg little creative/artistic for the more able, little science for the less able, many practical courses of a similar nature, especially for girls); the notion of 'balance' trivialised to mean a collection of certain types of subjects; and little focus given to moral questions, political literacy, environmental education, cultural diversity, adult and working life (cf HMI, 1984). Inadequacy in the curriculum offer will be reflected in a variety of pupil responses, and it is likely that one of these will be disruptive behaviour.

Moves toward a modular curriculum structure (eg ILEA, 1984) may be successful in improving motivation and increasing flexibility. If managed well the flexibility could also lead to a curriculum more applicable to adolescents' interests and life-views.

Examination of the learning offer cannot be divorced from an examination of the learning–teaching processes which are used: curriculum engages pedagogy. This is an area that the pastoral team may have been slow to consider, yet it is clearly the case that the overall pattern of teaching methods used in a school will bear a relation to the patterns of discipline. In one of their illuminating studies monitoring disruptive incidents (which will be referred to repeatedly in this chapter), Lawrence, Steed and Young (1981) present the following table from a study of an 11–18 co-educational school. In one week's monitoring, incidents in classrooms occurred while the type of teaching was as shown:

Whole class	30
Group work	3
Individual work	17
Whole-class and individual work	2
Other	4
	56

At first sight this would seem to be striking evidence for the connection between indiscipline and particular teaching methods. We consider this would be a likely plausible conclusion. However, there is some possibility that the large number of disruptive incidents during whole-class teaching merely reflects the possibility that whole-class teaching was used a great deal in that school that week, in which case, we could not directly conclude that disruptiveness was related to teaching methods. Even if we have no information as to how much each of these methods were used in that week, this data would certainly suggest to any teacher that it could be profitable to investigate a possible connection between methods of teaching and classroom management. This discussion will be taken further in the next chapter.

The use of more flexible teaching methods is recognised by HMI as one of the major national priorities for in-service training (Tomlinson, 1980).

'Most classroom conversations consist of questions from the

teacher, evoking short answers from the pupils, and few schools consistently encourage pupils to develop arguments; to formulate as well as answer questions; and to articulate their ideas through more open discussion . . . Among the less able, although many are interested and industrious, about half seem to find little purpose in their work . . . Almost invariably the tasks which are set are too closely directed by the teacher. In fourth and fifth year classes especially, much of the teaching and learning is narrowly focused on what teachers perceive, sometimes wrongly, to be the requirements of public examinations. As a consequence, approaches to work in the classroom are assiduous but over-cautious.' (HMI, 1984)

There is much room for development here, and the pastoral team has an important role to play. Lest they hold back through anticipation of being accused of treading on others' toes, we need only remember that as subject teachers too they will be treading on their own toes. Perhaps this will encourage an appropriate degree of sensitivity all round. In many cases the members of the pastoral team are in a good position to stimulate the review of teaching methods, since they have already been involved with the ideas and approaches through the development of more active approaches to teaching and learning in the pastoral curriculum (some aspects of which are considered in Chapter 5). Where this is the case, the obvious trap for them is to forget their sensitivity and to become 'crusaders' for active methods, unwittingly generating polarisations between staff and a lack of change as a result.

The processes involved in assessment may also illuminate patterns of disaffection and disruption. Pupils who receive regular, understandable, positive feedback regarding their performance on tasks they see the point of, are less likely to become disenchanted with their work. When effectively handled, self-assessment also has a potentially motivating result. Similarly, the better examples of profiling, which incorporate real discussion and negotiation, can enhance pupils' feelings of being in charge of their learning and development.

Finally, curricular arrangements for providing support to pupil learning can affect a school's pattern of disenchantment and indiscipline. Through a variety of routes all pupils can be helped to develop the skills of independent learning, extend their knowledge of how they learn best, and enhance the particular skills which are required to make the most of classroom life – these are major aspects of the pastoral curriculum. For all pupils, the way in which teaching is adjusted to their particular needs, abilities, language strengths and so on has an important bearing on their attentiveness and involvement. For those pupils who are deemed to require additional attention, the mechanism through which this is achieved can make the difference betwen an alienated adolescent who feels her/himself to be 'in the dumb class', and a persevering adolescent who welcomes occasional extra attention in her/his class from a helpful adult.

This final point anticipates the next section, which argues that the pastoral approach to analysing school discipline requires no pastoral/academic split.

Features of the school organisation and management

In this section some of the ways in which the school is administered will be mentioned for their potential effect on behaviour patterns.

The policy for grouping pupils is of major importance. At the start this includes the criteria according to which pupils are or are not placed in the same groups on entry to the first year. Examples still exist of this process being used in crude and doubtful ways which generate early disaffiliation from school – 'Those two were too friendly in primary school. We'll put them in different tutor groups.' Rather than accept the social dimension of school life and work with it profitably, some schools appear to want to organise it away.

Perhaps more obvious is the effect of grouping pupils by 'ability' – streaming and the like. In a study of a 14–18 urban boys' school, Lawrence, Steed and Young (1977) monitored disruptive incidents for two separate weeks, and showed the following pattern across ability 'bands':

Number of disruptive incidents

	Year 4	*Year 5*
Band 1	5	6
Band 2	11	19
Band 3	34	25

This pattern closely resembled that shown by noting the boys named in such incidents:

Number of pupils mentioned

	Year 4	*Year 5*
Band 1	9	7
Band 2	5	20
Band 3	25	21

It would be naive in the extreme to say that a simple cause-effect relationship obtains here: banding cannot be said to cause disruption even though it can be said that greater disruption occurs in lower bands. But if we were to speculate on the pattern which might obtain under random grouping of pupils and therefore perhaps less polarising messages, it seems unlikely that more disruption would be associated with an even distribution. In the above example, which must have been at least a ten form entry upper school, fourth-year classes with four of the mentioned pupils in each might offer very different dynamics than the Band 3 classes with more than twice that number.

A change in the grouping policy would not necessarily generate an effect by itself. If we have mixed-ability grouping it must be accompanied by mixed-ability teaching methods. We do not underestimate the complex repertoire of skills required for teaching mixed-ability groups well, nor the particular resource organisation which is required. Nevertheless, there is evidence that ability grouping often leads to negative dynamics in the low status groups, which many teachers find difficult, especially with underdeveloped curriculum and resources. This process may be compounded by the effects of various other organisational policies: an example is given in the above research where the fourth-year Band 3 'appear to spend a lot of time together as a group: their identity may therefore be stronger than that of other groups'.

A school's timetable can be viewed as the organisation's statement about what activities are deemed appropriate, which achieve priority over others, which are best resourced in terms of space, staff, and so on. It is likely to embody patterns which are associated with the whole-school patterns in discipline. Extreme examples easily come to mind – low status subjects which are not helped from that position by being scheduled with difficult classes on a Friday afternoon – but the more subtle examples require closer investigation. The details of timetable construction are nowadays surrounded by such mystique that school staff often fail to take charge of this major feature of their organisation. Yet detailed investigation can reveal many possibilities for creative change.

The differential distribution of resources, and especially of space in the school buildings, can carry strong messages to pupils. An example is that of a school where three year heads share a partially converted toilet for their office! Similarly, other social messages which may be conveyed by the state of the school's physical environment need to be considered. Broken lockers, disfigured desks, incapacitated classroom equipment can contribute to an atmosphere of decay, and this can easily turn into a downward spiral. Yet the spiral can again become an upward one, through concerted effort over time by the staff, in the first instance, with positive effects on patterns of behaviour.

A second major feature of the school's organisation and management which will have effects on pupils' affiliation to and disaffiliation from school is the way in which pupils' responsibility is recognised and engaged through their participation in the organisation. There are numerous schools which do not attend to this aspect. Their underlying attitude toward pupils is to think of them in groups which spend their day travelling around a range of locations to have a range of processes applied to them – the parallel with a production system, with the student seen as a product in the making, is clear (Handy, 1984). Unlike the inanimate production-line object, however, pupils may display marked alienation, in an active manner. Schools which engage their pupils, take their views seriously and consult them in decision-making, and generally treat them more as clients than as products, may be doing much to foster a climate in which disaffection is reduced.

The effective pastoral team will also be concerned that the pupils learn how the school works as an organisation. To spend time discussing with pupils why the school works the way it does (without defensively portraying it in an over-rational way), how the systems have been developed, and the range of ways in which pupils can make use of it, is to invite their participation and engagement. Some suggestions for activities which may stimulate discussion on some of these themes are given in Chapter 5. Work of this sort is now widely recognised as valuable when pupils enter the school, choose subject options, and so on – this is reflected in the treatment of such themes in the pastoral curriculum – but such discussions with pupils will be meaningful only if the school really has openings for the pupils to play their part, alongside the staff.

Features of the staff

It would be contradictory on the part of any pastoral team to pay great attention to the needs and position of pupils without also giving attention to the needs and position of staff. The fact that this does occur on occasion is, in our view, because some tutors are not completely attuned to pupil needs: they are simply siding with their perception of the pupil's position and have yet to develop the empathy towards staff which they may apparently show towards pupils. The feelings, satisfactions and aspirations of the staff group are of crucial importance in understanding the successes of a school. Many take this position, including Gillham (1984) who says:

'. . . if a school has to be a psychologically satisfying and secure place for children, it also has to be so for teachers. To a large extent, the two sets of conditions will be the same, because interactive: satisfied pupils will, by and large, mean satisfied teachers.'

When we consider aspects of the school which are associated with patterns of disruption we must consider staff support systems.

'A supportive structure for teachers within the school organisation, and a programme of in-service training to enable them to develop class-management strategies and air their difficulties without embarrassment, has to be part of any comprehensive attempt to minimise conflict and reduce its destructive consequences.' (Gillham, 1984)

A group which meets regularly, at a comfortable time and place, perhaps with an outside consultant, and which develops discussion of classroom management, will prove invaluable to colleagues, whether or not they have extended experience. It will be one element in overcoming the isolation of teachers in their classrooms, however successful. The contents of the next chapter may provide some input or structure to the discussion. Such a group will occasionally need to review its own functioning, and will become a feature of the school which deserves organisational support. More structured INSET sessions on classroom management will also deserve inclusion in the school's development programme. A further element will be the constructive use of already existing team meetings, some of whose time can be devoted to examining the available information on the school's patterns of behaviour.

Here we are beginning to raise an important general theme: the styles and channels of communication between staff. From the most immediate examples, where good communication is required in crisis situations, to the most extended, where open communication is required to foster reflection and discussion of the school's practices, the quality of communication between staff will be crucial. As another barometer of the school as an organisation, more or less effective staff communication will doubtless be mirrored in more or less disrupting behaviour. Resources (including those of time and money) devoted to improving the channels and styles of communication are likely to be profitable investments in schools, where communication is often fragmented and interrupted as the task of management is attempted in teachers' spare time.

If positive support, meetings and communication are features of positive staff dynamics, the opposite can be evidenced through negative staff attitudes, high turnover rates and so on, which can be associated with high pupil disaffection. Negative staff attitudes, either towards particular pupils or towards particular groups (ethnic, gender or class), are often barely visible to the outside observer yet are picked up quickly by pupils and resisted in a variety of active or passive ways. To a significant extent the presence of such attitudes in a staff group is connected to the levels of overall satisfaction/dissatisfaction in the group, and it can be profitable to take this overall view when examining whole-school levels of discipline. The turnover rate amongst a staff group can bear a similar connection. In Reynolds' (1977) study of nine South Wales schools, 15% of the total variance in the attendance rates of the schools was accounted for by the variable of staff turnover (which bore an even stronger connection to the measures of academic attainment). This aspect of a staff, however, does not so much reflect the communication between staff – as did others discussed earlier in this section – rather it reflects something about the coherence of the system at large.

Features of the school as a social system

Here we first note the conclusion by Bird and colleagues (1980) to their study of disaffected pupils in six schools:

> 'One characteristic of a climate favourable to the working through of appropriate responses to disaffected behaviour was what, for want of a better term we identify as staff coherence. In contrast to other schools . . . some schools were grappling with their institutional problems in coherent and consistent fashions. There was no single model of staff coherence, nor a simple explanation of how it functioned in any one school . . . Coherence should not however be confused with uniformity. Many personal styles and differentiated skills can be exhibited within a coherent staff team.'
> (Bird *et al*, 1980)

This quality of coherence is no doubt built up over a period of time and reflects much about a school's practices for working together: team-work perhaps of a cross-curricular nature. It is unlikely to be imposed – that would be uniformity or conformity of a superficial nature. Its opposite is akin to the difficult school described by Lawrence *et al* (1984) in which the environment has come to feel unstructured, with apparently random irregularities to the programme of school life, and with the general instability triggering off incidents which themselves perpetuate the instability. This description suggests that the feeling of coherence in a school may well be associated with another important quality, that of purposefulness.

Schools convey their own brand of purposefulness in a variety of ways, through numerous aspects of their activity. But the point being made here is that different schools (and different parts of a school) may convey more or less of that sense of purposefulness and direction. Some of the aspects which the research of Rutter *et al* (1979) identified as associated with a school's overall behaviour rating make a combined sense under this heading: attitude of teachers toward academic aims, setting and marking of homework, staff timekeeping at beginning and end of lessons, and the use of praise for good behaviour in and out of class. These features should not be viewed rigidly, as though conformity to them would directly ease misbehaviour: they should be viewed as indicators through which the message of purposefulness can be communicated.

In a school which is characterised by coherence and purposefulness there will be differences among teachers but not divides in the staff. As Jones (1984) suggests, the ability of senior management to handle complex situations will be mirrored in the ability of the staff to do the same (including the skill of coping with the many complications which may arise through the exercise of any style of authority, and the skills of resolving conflict). Heads and teachers will then be effective in the important task of preventing difficulties from arising and, on the occasions when they do occur, preventing an over-reaction from dominating the life of the school. The pastoral team have a crucial part to play here.

The particular aims which are espoused to help the system's purposefulness will vary from school to school, as different social contexts and conditions have effect. But almost invariably these purposes will relate to the major influences around the school – parents, community, employers, and so on. This demonstrates another feature of the school as a social system – how high or low are its boundaries with salient aspects of its environment. Some secondary schools still seem to show their monastic heritage through their lack of contact with the immediate world around them. It is more likely that a school which can show its pupils that its purposes connect to a wider environment and to the pupils' goals and aspirations will achieve lower whole-school levels of indiscipline.

A final point, with some similarity to the last mentioned, focuses on the position of teachers. They, too, will probably reflect the degree of success with which the school relates to the outside world and perhaps in particular the educational world. Coherence and purposefulness for them may be linked to the school's keeping in touch with educational development through a variety of channels, so that it knowingly thinks ahead, anticipates changes in its environment, and plans rather than merely reacting. It is likely that this process will test out other aspects of the school as an organisation: some schools may be arranged in such a way that they can cope with more extensive rates of change. But all schools have their limits, especially for externally initiated change, and if this limit is reached or surpassed in a school then the coherence and purposefulness become overstretched, and pupil behaviour suffers.

At this point we will end the discussion of whole-school features which relate to patterns of indiscipline, in order to move to the particular applied question – how to work positively with such patterns in a particular school. The preceding discussion has attempted to order a wide range of potential influences which the pastoral team may have to consider, investigate, and address with colleagues. We have included those for which there seems to be supporting evidence in research and other literature (and may have left out some of our personal 'favourites').

But which will be relevant to your school?

'Where do I start in my school?'

Each school has its own characteristic level and pattern of indiscipline which may reflect some of the features discussed above. These features may be reflected through the overall levels (how much) as a whole-school phenomenon, and/or through the patterns (where located and where not) as a within-school phenomenon.

But how may such patterns be examined and brought forward for discussion in a school? We suggest an approach which has three main components:

- gathering data in the school;
- setting up a problem-solving group for this work;
- extensive ongoing negotiation of methods and outcomes with concerned colleagues.

Each will now be outlined before the first is examined in detail.

Many of the occasions when a school staff discusses discipline are not characterised by the examination of data on the issue which has been collected in the school. Accordingly, these occasions are more likely to be characterised by members of staff putting forward their own personal beliefs about the causes and control of indiscipline than they are by joint problem-solving. Since personal beliefs on this theme are rarely developed through collection of factual data (as Chapter 1 implied) and are more likely to embody the whole range of individual emotional positions, such occasions are often dogged by a greater proportion of non-rational processes than may be profitable. The introduction of some sort of data into such debates can bring both realistic structure and forward direction to the discussion. This, of course, will depend on who introduces it and how it is done.

Single members of staff attempting to generate and introduce such data stand a good chance of experiencing the fate of most hero/heroine innovators – their efforts sacrificed to the larger processes of the organisational system (Georgiades and Phillimore, 1975). It is important that such work is done by a group of colleagues. They will gain extra strength from the range of perspectives they bring, and will act as an important model of working, in contrast to the norm of school life that teachers do not discuss behaviour problems in a group of peers. Ideally, the composition of the group would reflect the various criteria for staff credibility in the school and would include a range of pastoral/academic, high/low formal status, informal groupings and so on.

Any working group in a school staff can fall into the trap of becoming perceived as a clique. To avoid this and, more important, to ensure that the approach taken to the work is successful, energy must be invested in maintaining continual open communication within the school, negotiating the detail of information-gathering with all the staff concerned. Many of the approaches to gathering data require that colleagues provide information and their perspective. Therefore any working group must negotiate the plans, the ways of collecting information and, most importantly, its intended use, with all concerned.

Methods of deriving information on behaviour patterns

In many schools there are already sets of information which reflect patterns of discipline/indiscipline, but there is sometimes a need to gather further clear information.

In a school where the pastoral team is used for coping with discipline issues, the data inherent in the pattern of referrals to that team can be illuminative and powerful. For a head of year/house to record and organise this information, showing its relation to such features as subject of lesson, style of work, referring teacher, year-group of pupil, etc, is an important first step. In many cases the feeding in of such information to informal discussions with the appropriate subject departments can achieve the required result of reviewing their practice. On other occasions the dissemination of such information around the school has been known to stimulate a wider debate, albeit one which may start from a more heated beginning.

In a school where a special unit is operating in an attempt to cope with pupils whose effect is disruptive, the pattern of referrals to that unit may again illuminate some of the wider patterns and influences on pupil behaviour. In the previous chapter (p 18) we outlined our reservations regarding the use of units for such purposes – it follows that when a unit is operating in what we would regard as a distorted way (especially when the aims and referral methods are not firmly agreed and adhered to as we outlined earlier), the data about who is referred is likely to say something about aspects other than the pupils, for example year-group, subject department, curriculum offer, referring teacher, and so on. The careful use of this data by teachers running the unit or by the pastoral team can be an extra element in directing the debate to some of these aspects.

A considerable range of methods for gathering new information is available. The most informal or unstructured technique is increasingly known by its evocative title of 'pupil pursuit'. Here, a teacher undertakes the task of experiencing the lessons taken by a particular pupil or group of pupils, usually for a complete day. The style of observation is inactive, ie not engaging with the classroom activity, and the focus of observation may to some degree be clarified beforehand. Such an exercise, carefully written up to bring out the school-level issues, can provide another useful input to more general staff discussions, at the same time being a useful staff development activity for the individual observer.

More structured methods, which may also satisfy those who seek quantifiable results, may be effective on occasion. A notable set of results has been generated by Lawrence, Steed and Young (1977, 1981) who use a technique for monitoring disruptive incidents by means of teachers' self-reports of incidents they themselves experience. This avoids the difficulties involved in observing other teachers' classrooms, and maintains the important element of teacher interpretation, which is essential to understanding patterns of deviance. Clearly, the use of such an approach will require much time spent on detailed negotiation with all staff: when the monitoring will take place, how long for, how information is to be recorded, how information is to be collected and most of all the purpose and the intended analysis – all these will need

Figure 2.1

Disruptive Incident Report Form

This is the form which was agreed for collecting information on incidents you regard as disruptive. Please fill in as much of the information as you are reasonably able to do, and return the completed sheet in the agreed way.

Day/Date

Period/Time

Teaching group

Subject being taught

Room or place

Your description of the incident
   (continue on the back of this form if needed)

Number of pupils involved

Names of pupils involved

How did the incident end?

Please describe any action you took

Your name
   (or the confidential staff number agreed for this exercise)

                                                        Thank you

discussion and agreement. It is likely that a 'circular' definition of disruption as discussed in Chapter 1 will attract agreement amongst staff: behaviour which interferes seriously with the teaching process and/or seriously upsets the normal running of the school (cf p 10). The method of recording incidents can be simple and straightforward, as Figure 2.1 shows.

Because of the reservations which teachers still have about describing disruption in their classes, the number of incidents recorded will probably be an underestimate of the total. Nevertheless, the pattern of results over whatever period has been chosen will reveal something of the school's overall patterns.

When the working group has collected all the reports from the monitoring period, it is likely that a written report will be useful for staff to consider. At this stage much care must be devoted to the description of results and especially any apparent explanation of results, for spurious but apparently plausible explanations may enter, some of which serve to divert attention from the school processes and the context of the behaviour. Take this example: a school monitors disruptive incidents for one week and notices an increase in incidents reported in the middle of the week. The write-up of results suggests that this may be explained by staff stress increasing and tolerance reducing towards Wednesday, whereas after Wednesday stress is dispersed by the prospect of the weekend. This explanation may sound plausible, but note that it is an explanation in terms of the structure of a five-day working week: it says nothing about the particular school (and should therefore apply equally to all schools). The fact is that other schools have markedly different patterns across the days of the week. Another school finds that it has almost a third of its disruptive incidents reported on Monday, declining towards Wednesday and staying at that level. Therefore, we cannot adopt an explanation which omits any mention of the school itself.

As a general principle in writing up results of monitoring it is appropriate to say that any attempts at explanation should first relate to aspects of the school, its organisation, curriculum, staff and climate.

A further point regarding the explanation of results applies to the written report and to the discussions amongst staff: the main aim of a monitoring exercise is not to explain patterns of pupil behaviour but to identify patterns and set up more focused investigations. For example, a popular suburban school set up a monitoring exercise for a week, with some staff privately hoping that the results would bring about a change in breaktime schedules and duties. In fact, only 2% of disruptive incidents occurred outside lesson time, and 33 lessons during the week were disrupted for their full duration. Thus the monitoring led to an examination of curriculum suitability, alongside staff INSET in classroom management and in pastoral care. This school's experience also demonstrates the amount of time taken to negotiate a monitoring exercise: from first formal mention of the idea to written report for staff took one year.

Finally, if the analysis of monitoring results is carried out in the way suggested, it is likely to lead to further explorations at all three levels: whole-school, classroom and individual pupil. As in the order of chapters in this book, it is important to give an initial focus to the whole-school perspective, mainly to counteract the tendency to individualise in discussions of deviance. But the other two levels of classroom and individual will also show through any monitoring results. In examining classroom and individual patterns the principle of keeping the context in mind must prevail.

Summary

This chapter has focused on the whole-school level of analysis. Different schools show different patterns of pupil behaviour, and this reflects differences in their informal climate and culture. The counter-productive effects of a polarising ethos and of a rigid rule climate were discussed. Regular rule reviews can be productive at the whole-school level.

Differences within a school also contribute to the patterns of pupil behaviour. Four areas were discussed: first, flexibility and applicability of curriculum together with flexibility of teaching methods, assessment and support for learning; second, organisational policies such as the grouping of pupils, timetabling, distribution of resources and involvement of pupils in decision-making; third, staff considerations such as support systems, communication levels, attitudes and turnover; fourth, wider features of the school system, its coherence and purposefulness, and how these relate to its wider environment.

An intervention on these school patterns can be initiated by a working group of staff who negotiate the gathering of information and its discussion by staff. A range of methods was mentioned, and a particular focus was given to the monitoring of disruptive incidents.

Suggestions for discussion/investigation

1 How would you characterise the climate of the school in which you work? Share your thoughts on this with a number of colleagues who work in different teams and with those in your own pastoral and academic teams.
2 How would you characterise the culture of the organisation in which you work? (cf p 39). Discuss this, together with any strengths and weaknesses you identify, with a number of other staff members.
3 How would you describe the climate of rule application in your school? Interview about six pupils to see whether they regard the enforcement of some rules as counter-productive. Are there some rules for which a general 'truce' has been agreed? (cf p 42).
4 What is your impression of the within-school patterns of indiscipline in your school? Does this pattern relate to curriculum, organisation, staff and so on? (cf pp 45–54).
5 If you are a head of year/house/pastoral section, keep a record of pupils sent to you for disciplinary reasons (cf p 55). Discuss this record with two colleagues who are also pastoral team leaders and with two colleagues who are heads of subject sections.
6 Start some informal discussions on monitoring disruptive incidents in your school. Prepare a short paper on the idea, including all the aspects which would need to be negotiated, and start to discuss the identification of possible members of a working group for the task.

3   The whole-class perspective

Outline

This chapter considers the situation which most involves teachers' and pupils' time – the classroom. There are important and distinctive features which characterise the classroom situation – these are considered before moving on to ways of thinking about the behaviour of pupils and teachers in and across these situations. Is there such a phenomenon as an ill-disciplined class? If so, how may we tackle such an issue? What notions and practices can help us understand pupils' roles in classroom groups? What are the connections with the teaching approach and how may we most profitably start to talk about these connections with colleagues? In raising these questions this chapter aims to indicate positive practices at the *classroom* level of analysis.

The classroom situation – setting the scene

In this chapter we will make good use of ideas which draw attention to the classroom situation. Why should this be so? When we hear about behaviour in classrooms, we tend to hear about the people involved – Jill did such and such, and the teacher did so and so. We rarely hear about the situation, the context in which the behaviour occurs, so we end up with a partial picture of behaviour, as though it occurred independently of its context. Part of the reason for this may be that our language generally has a structure which does not help us talk as fluently about situations as about people: it sounds clumsy to say 'In the context of x our interaction was y'. Indeed, some attempts to talk about situations can sound like gobbledygook on first hearing, and others are good material for jokes, as in 'an on-going teacher–learner interaction situation'. Nevertheless, it is a striking fact that our everyday language about teaching contains so little analysis of the classroom as a distinctive social situation. The same can be said for the formal and research literature – perhaps this explains why decades of research on teachers has minimal impact in terms of changing classrooms.

The situation has a considerable influence and needs to be understood if we are to make sense of behaviour in classrooms. This point applies whether we are referring to pupil behaviour or to teacher behaviour. As an example of the latter, in their study of teachers' classroom management strategies in Scottish secondary schools, Corrie *et al* (1982) concluded:

'It is evident that much of the distinctive character of the teachers' strategies for handling interaction in the classroom was derived from the nature of the context in which they worked, comprising both the immediate situation in the classroom itself and the organisational setting of the schools within which such strategies were employed.'

As we intend to show in the first part of this chapter, there are two major positive gains available for teachers when they examine the classroom situation more carefully. The first is that it can 'take the heat off' the individual teacher who would otherwise, erroneously, be seen as the only influence in the classroom – in doing this, it could provide a much-needed antidote to over-personalised and over-individualised accounts of classroom events (including the inappropriate labelling of teachers in a variety of ways). The second is that if teachers work from a perspective which examines the classroom situation, they may develop an additional set of possibilities for achieving their teaching goals. In other words, we can take a positive view on the influence of the situation, by ensuring to arrange it in the service of our educational purposes. A third, more long-term gain could be that if teachers themselves are able to communicate the complexity of the classroom to a wider audience, we may encounter less often the view that a lay-person could manage it equally well!

We will start our perspective on classrooms by attempting to grasp their complex and busy nature, the very nature which makes them demanding and sometimes stressful environments.

Through a similar consideration, when we attempt to understand the behaviour of pupils, it is necessary to understand the context. This perspective will be carried through in the following chapter where the focus is on the individual pupil. In both chapters we shall utilise the fact that pupils in secondary schools spend their day in a range of situations (ie different lessons in the main), and we can therefore highlight how their behaviour is linked to the context by conducting a sort of survey across a range of lessons. Through this process we will avoid the tendency to locate the causes of behaviour 'inside' persons and the associated tendency for teachers to feel powerless about change unless the person of the pupil somehow changes.

These points refer to classroom behaviour generally and to disruptive behaviour in particular. Our focus on the situation applies there too. For example, if we are to discuss what is commonly called classroom control, we shall not answer the question 'Who's in control of the classroom?' by referring solely to the teacher. It will not suffice merely to add that pupils are to some extent in control of the classroom. The important consideration is that the classroom situation is a controlling feature of behaviour, and it follows that a teacher's handling of the classroom context can be a powerful feature in influencing disruptive behaviour.

Here is an example of context in concrete terms;

The Governor of a New York prison was worried about the amount of fighting between inmates. The strategy of 'change the person', by putting fighters on a bread and water diet, seemed ineffective. So did the more liberal version: talking to fighting inmates to persuade them into better behaviour. The problem was finally solved by calling in a bricklayer, who rounded off the walls at the junctions of corridors – these had been identified as the situations where fighting broke out, when poor visibility led to surprise encounters.

This story focuses on only one aspect of a situation: its physical dimensions. These are important in their influence on behaviour even though they do not paint the whole picture. In classrooms, too, the physical arrangements have an effect. Even before everyone arrives in a classroom, observation of these arrangements can confirm the remark made by one researcher – 'settings have plans for their inhabitants' behaviour' (Barker, 1963).

When a classroom is filled with pupils and teacher(s), the physical arrangements have an effect on the next and arguably most important consideration – the social arrangements. By this we mean the particular ways in which the teacher will enact their role on that occasion, and the particular ways in which the pupils will enact their roles on that occasion. The possibilities are many and varied: what will be the pattern of ways in which the various people work together, interact and interrelate? Will they work alone, in pairs, in groups? Will they need to help each other, talk, co-operate? Through these social arrangements the various people develop a view of their role and a view of their contribution to the learning process.

Brian the drama teacher has a large open space in his drama room. He arranges chairs in pairs throughout the room and sets the class off on their warm-up activity while he keeps time. The pupils view themselves as active users of their out-of-school knowledge and the teacher views himself as facilitator and monitor. Sheila the science teacher has a laboratory with fixed furniture and resources. Having taught pupils how to use these, she splits the class into small groups to carry out investigations. The pupils see themselves as responsible problem-solvers and she views herself as an extra resource. Andrew teaches languages from the front of a classroom fitted with rows of desks and uses the blackboard for exercises which are then written by pupils individually.

The pupils see themselves as relatively inactive receivers of initially non-predictable knowledge, while Andrew sees himself as the sole source of this knowledge. These examples are not given in order to support any particular view of what teaching certain subjects should be like (indeed, many of the views which assert that particular subjects need to be taught in particular ways are based on questionable stereotypes). But perhaps these examples suggest how much of a classroom can be portrayed through a sentence or two which focuses on features of the situation.

Taking this further, there are aspects of the classroom situation which are less easily described but which are equally important in understanding the behaviour in that context. These not-so-obvious aspects will now be examined, together with their implications for teachers and for pupils. When the complete picture of the situation has been built up we can proceed to an understanding of disruptive behaviour, at the same time having a framework available for arranging the classroom situation so as to avoid creating unnecessary difficulty.

There follow five statements which describe aspects of classrooms. The analysis owes much to the work of Doyle (1980), Jackson (1968) and Kounin (1976).

1   Classrooms are busy places

Teachers can be engaged in 1000 interactions a day. It is very difficult to name a comparable job on this dimension. One result of this for the teacher can, of course, be tiredness, especially for the beginner teacher, or even stress. This feature also draws to our attention the fact that because events happen fast teachers learn to act fast: their appraisal and decision-making in classrooms is rapid. Even so, every event cannot be reflected on in depth, so the development of routines is another feature of classroom life which helps cope with the busy-ness of the situation. From a pure 'education' viewpoint some routines may embody poor practice for the sake of pupil learning, but the classroom situation makes such demands. If teachers do not typically reflect in significant depth on the pupil's perspective in classrooms (as is confirmed by research such as that by Stebbins, 1976) we should expect their professional reflections to take place at less busy times outside the classroom, unless special strategies can be devised to create time for this purpose in class.

For the pupils in this busy environment it is apparent (and confirmed by numerous classroom interaction studies) that the amount of individual attention they receive with the teacher in a day is likely to be only a few minutes and probably highly interrupted. The way in which we make sense of learning in classrooms must take this into account by not implying that pupils learn when interacting with teachers. Pupils have to get used to being one of many, especially when it comes to adult attention, and this can demand extra skills of being able to wait.

2 Classrooms are public places

This statement is meant in two ways. First, classrooms are public in the general sense that many people have a view or opinion on classrooms and how they ought to operate. Second, classrooms are public in that a teacher's and a pupil's behaviour is generally highly visible to all the other members in the event.

The implication of the first for the teacher is that s/he can be thought of as at the centre of a number of people's expectations – parents, colleagues, head, local authority, central government and, of course, pupils. In the unlikely event that these various expectations are in broad agreement with each other the teacher will probably feel strongly supported in her/his job. It is more likely that disagreements exist and the teacher feels in a state of 'role strain'. Resolving role strain can be accomplished in a number of ways, each with its own costs and benefits – a classic has been the strategy of isolating role performance from view by the conflicting parties: the classroom as a castle, with paper over the windows to the corridor.

The implication of the second sense of publicness are various: teachers may feel that they are on stage to some degree, teachers may act toward one pupil with the intention of affecting others in the audience, but mainly teachers adopt a focus toward groups of pupils (whole class or less). This group focus grows out of the imbalance in numbers in the classroom and also serves to cope with the busy-ness of the situation.

The publicness of classrooms means that pupils experience much public evaluation of their work and behaviour and they adopt a variety of strategies in the face of this (strategies to work out what answer teacher wants, strategies to assess whether teacher is being fair in her/his evaluations, and so on). Some studies suggest that teachers give public evaluations of pupils every few minutes. A final feature of this publicness of classrooms is that pupils experience being treated as a member of a group which is not always of their choosing and in turn may adopt a group approach toward affecting others (including on occasion their teacher).

3 Classroom events are multi-dimensional

This statement reminds us that there is a wide variety of different purposes, interests and goals represented by the different personnel in a classroom. Teaching and learning are but one dimension, the appointed aspect, of the events and processes. The social and personal aspects of pupils, the livelihood and personal aspects of teachers set off multiple reverberations with each other and with the appointed task. Even when we focus on the learning dimension alone the statement still applies. The classroom contains a multiplicity of information sources (books, worksheets, displays, other visuals, as well as all the verbal and non-verbal behaviour of teachers and pupils), and these sources generally do not all refer to the same thing. Indeed, as well as being incompatible, the information in a classroom is also not consistent, even when it comes to deciding what learning task is required. A problematic environment!

For the teacher an implication is that they need to manage events on a multiplicity of dimensions: knowing subject, appraising students, managing classroom groups, coping with emotional responses to events, establishing procedures, distributing resources, keeping records and so on. With these tasks all affecting each other the result may feel overwhelming on occasion (most likely if they are seen as 'interfering' with a superordinate interest in managing subject matter).

For pupils this multidimensional environment means that on the occasion when they intend to engage in academic work they need to display considerable skills selecting what is salient information and what is not, especially when attempting to identify the demands of a task. (These are not usually the skills which are referred to when identifying academic achievement).

4   Classroom events are simultaneous

The multiple tasks and dimensions in the classroom do not occur in a step-by-step fashion but simultaneously, especially from the teacher's point of view. While one pupil is immersed in activity, another is just finishing, a third requires some help. Teachers attend to numerous aspects at the same time: the pace of work, the sequencing of pupil contributions, the distribution of pupils attended to, the accuracy of pupil contributions, the development of the argument, and so on, while at the same time monitoring work involvement levels, other pupil behaviours and external events.

This has at least two implications for teachers. First, it is important to exercise the skill (at least apparently) of being able to monitor more than one aspect at once. This is sometimes characterised as the 'eyes in the back of the head' phenomenon. Second, it follows that teachers may exercise a choice as to which aspect to respond to and which to ignore. The style of operation of this choice can have critical effects and can make the difference between a 'smooth' teaching performance which gives rise to a purposeful climate, and a 'lumpy' performance where the teacher seems controlled by events and appears to be 'chopping and changing'.

For the pupils the simultaneity of classroom events is not such a salient phenomenon since they may not intend to have a perspective on the whole situation and its events. However, the fact that it is salient for teachers can be exploited very effectively by those waiting for teacher's back to turn.

5 Classroom events are unpredictable

This statement draws attention to the fact that in such a busy multidimensional environment it is not possible to be in a position of predicting the course of events with a fine degree of accuracy. It reminds us of two sorts of phenomena in classrooms. The first is the considerable disruptive effect of interruptions, either external (the window cleaner, the snowstorm) or internal (the projector breakdown, the Tannoy announcement). The second is the importance which teachers give to being able to predict, for example, pupils' responses to work, pacing of work, other aspects of pupil behaviour. Further, the importance of establishing routines in classroom life can be seen as one attempt to bring predictability to the situation and to reduce the ambiguity.

This statement has power for the pupil's perspective too. It is possible to note a variety of strategies which pupils may adopt to reduce the ambiguity of some academic tasks, for example, asking the teacher to be very specific in what is expected, using strategies for divining what answer the teacher wants to the question, and opting for low-risk predictable tasks when choice is given.

Finally, it is possible to see both teachers and pupils attempting to make each other more predictable through the process of categorising, labelling and stereotyping. This becomes understandable in some ways when we see it in the context of a busy, multidimensional, unpredictable situation – the classroom. In that context it is perhaps less than surprising that people adopt partial and limited views of each other. But it does not follow that these views will necessarily maintain elsewhere, for example, on the part of teachers discussing their pupils during a meeting. And it will be even less likely that the stereotypes generated in the classroom will maintain if pupils and teachers meet and get to know each other in a wider range of contexts (in school, on residential experiences, in the community, at home).

Where does this perspective lead?

By recognising the highly complex nature of the classroom situation it is more likely that recognition of the highly complex nature of the teacher's job will follow. This is certainly more likely than if we were to conceptualise the teacher's task on the basis of models drawn from thinking about *a* teacher and *a* pupil with little reference to context (ie many 'learning' theories), or if we were to jump into talking about supposedly different 'styles' of teaching such as authoritarian/democratic or informal/formal (ie the polarisations which on occasion litter teacher talk and some of the formal literature). These views of the teacher's task are trivialisations of that complex task because they do not explicitly (or implicitly) consider the context in which teaching takes place. The demands on teachers which are generated by the characteristics of the classroom are demands faced by *all* teachers: they are unavoidable and central.

From this perspective it is possible to see the fundamental skills of teaching as:

a managing the classroom setting.

b managing the demands generated by the classroom situation.

Under *a* would be included the management of the physical setting (an aspect over which many teachers feel that they have little choice) and the interrelated aspect of the social structure of the classroom (how pupils are grouped and how they work together). Under *b* would be included the skills necessary to handle the features of classrooms which have been described above. Briefly, these can be seen as:

> *busy:* the ability to control timing effectively and smoothly, keeping a good pace to events, and to devise effective routines
>
> *public:* the ability to give a purposeful and personable self-presentation despite role-strain; the adoption of a focus on groups of pupils rather than individuals; the ability to involve class members in classroom events and to spread participation widely
>
> *multidimensional:* the ability to show awareness of the range of things happening in the classroom, and sometimes the interrelationship between them, and events outside the classroom
>
> *simultaneous:* the ability to manage two or more classroom events at the same time (and by implication to monitor two or more events at once), and to choose which events to ignore
>
> *unpredictable:* the ability to tolerate the ambiguity of the situation, and to set up routines which serve their ordering function without becoming restrictive or limiting.

The overall picture of the teacher is that of a skilled manager of a unique environment, an orchestrator of learning whose main task is that of planning, selecting and arranging *activities*. Writers such as Doyle (1980) are not being cynical or critical in arguing that 'from a management perspective a teacher's immediate task is to gain and maintain the cooperation of students in activities that fill classroom time'. This statement has considerable resonance with the question 'What shall I get them to do?' posed by many teachers and perhaps most vividly by learner teachers and substitute teachers. 'If any learning is to occur from teaching, the teacher must sustain cooperation of the student in an activity. To ignore this is to ignore the essence of teaching.' (Doyle, 1979) The student cooperation being talked of here is not necessarily with the teacher or with other pupils, but with the activity and at its most passive may mean the willingness to allow an activity to continue.

The perspective which develops from an analysis of the classroom situation reminds us that *planning activities* is the central skill of the teacher. This involves much more than stating objectives and choosing a method of instruction: it involves planning the social arrangements, forms of pupil behaviour, timing, and the non-academic aspects of the classroom.

So what about classroom discipline?

Two important implications can be derived from this perspective.

1 Whole class disruption is a rare event with distinctive characteristics

That fact that it is rare follows from the recognition that classrooms are such complex multidimensional environments that to get all the pupils acting in consort would be unlikely to occur by chance, and it also follows that the precursors to such an event are likely to be identifiable. These will be discussed in later sections of this chapter.

This implication is not intended to negate the experience of teachers who feel that a whole class is disruptive (usually it's 3R!) but to signal that on many of the occasions when we feel this way it transpires on closer investigation that many pupils are not involved. On these occasions it may be that high-visibility pupils are 'stealing the scene'. Methods of illuminating the roles they may be playing will also be examined later.

2 The most effective element in reducing general classroom disruption is the teacher's skill in planning activities

This implication is supported by research findings such as those of

Kounin (1976), whose extensive and detailed studies showed that the action which teachers took in response to a discipline problem had no consistent relationship with their managerial success. However, what teachers did *before* misbehaviour occurred was shown to be crucial in achieving success. The teacher's ability to manage the classroom group through planned activities is a key element.

It is worth noting that this approach is more likely to offer creative solutions than are the many approaches which focus on various aspects of the teacher's response to unwelcome behaviour. These latter often reflect the question which may be heard in many unstructured teacher conversations about discipline: 'What do I do if . . .?' or 'What do you do about . . .?' The inherent risk is that of casting the teacher in a response-led role, which is exactly what we have earlier identified as an ineffective strategy in the classroom situation. When some aspects of the teacher's response are raised later in this chapter it is with recognition of their secondary importance to the skills of planning activities.

For the pastoral team a further implication is that expertise about what is termed pedagogy must be developed and demonstrated if the pastoral team is to contribute significantly to debate about classroom discipline.

Now that we have set up our perspective on the classroom situation and classroom activities, we can go on to examine those particular behaviours which are the cause for concern in that context – disruptive behaviour. In line with the overall structure of this book, and its progression from large-scale to small-scale, the next two sections will examine whole-class disruption and part-class disruption.

Whole-class disruption?

'That class was awful today' is a comment which many teachers will have heard (and may have used). As was suggested earlier, such a comment does not necessarily reflect a cool analysis of a class's behaviour; it is more likely to have been delivered in the staffroom at breaktime, and thus serves the cathartic function of letting off steam in the context of a particular audience. Seen in this light, those with an additional concern for classroom discipline need not feel it necessary to initiate immediate action (and may be encouraged to continue stirring their coffee?).

These points should not be taken to deny that on occasion a whole class (or effectively the whole class) may present a reasonably unified response to something which in turn frustrates the teacher's goals.

Three general conditions can apply, each with different implications for action.

It may be that a class is generating difficulties because of the curriculum offering, especially if that offering is viewed as demeaning or devaluing. Examples of this are occasionally encountered when a school decides to create a different offering for 'lower ability groups' but then clearly gives inadequate resources of activities and motivated staff. On such occasions the pastoral team will hear similar critiques from pupils whose view of other aspects of school are more disparate. The pastoral team will thus be facing a particular case of the issues discussed in the preceding chapter, and their intervention will be similar to the style discussed there.

Second, it may be the case that a whole class is involved in difficulties with just one teacher: a quick survey of other teachers' perspectives by someone in the pastoral team would confirm or not. On such occasions it is most likely that some problematic features of the classroom climate can be quickly identified, and work may be undertaken with the teacher. The trap for the pastoral team in this situation is to believe that it could be easier to work with the class, either through cajoling them to be otherwise, or through threat. This is both impractical and unethical: impractical because any effects gained will be short lived since a major variable remains unchanged, and unethical because the teachers' accountability is not being addressed. Consequently, the pastoral team has to negotiate (in themselves and in others) those aspects of school culture which interpret direct work with colleagues as necessarily negative criticism, and demonstrate that helping is not something which requires to be preceded by blaming.

The process which can often be identified in classroom climates where a whole class is presenting difficulties to one teacher has a background history of conflict which has been built into the transactions for some time. A direct approach to creating change may not quickly generate results, and attention may be given to the aspects which *maintain* the present climate. Anonymity in the interpersonal relations is likely to be a feature: names are not used in addressing others and a situation of diffused responsibility can develop where the pupil's view is 'I'm not personally engaged in this, therefore it doesn't matter what I do'. An associated feature occurs where both pupils and teacher have ignored the more personal aspects of each other, the transactions take place on the restricted dimensions of work and order, and the interactions have become stereotypical. In both these cases the maintaining conditions of anonymity and stereotyping can be affected in order to recreate a situation where significant negotiation can occur. The use of personal names, and the reference to something other than task or control features of the classroom (but, of course, not highly personal topics) is likely to ease the situation to the extent that other change attempts introduced by the teacher have a better chance of being received realistically. It may also serve the purpose of giving the teacher the experience of success in introducing a change into the classroom, but not on the dimension which is central to any immediate conflict and is thus highly charged.

The third general condition which can be identified is an example of whole-class disruption wider than particular lessons or teacher: it applies when a class is presenting difficulties in a number of situations to a number of colleagues. In this instance it is likely that a particular reputation has been achieved by the class and allocated by some of the staff, and recognising this process is the key to positive change. Helping both pupils and teachers to understand the creation of reputations can put in their hands the power to undo them. Time needs to be set aside so that the whole class may discuss in a structured and detailed way the history and present functioning of their reputation. What particular aspects of this class have attracted attention? Why has such importance been attached to these aspects? What else has served to attract the present reputation? What are the advantages of this reputation to pupils, to teachers, and what are the disadvantages? What steps could be taken to change this reputation, and what potential barriers to change have to be anticipated? Which other people need to be engaged in this change attempt? These questions and others require reflection by both pupils and teachers, although it may not necessarily be best accomplished with the two groups together. Open investigation of the processes implies that pupils will be talking about their teachers and what they feel their teachers think of them, and suggesting why this is the case. This discussion may be most effectively facilitated by a teacher who is seen as credible by the class and has not been centrally involved in the difficulties which are being analysed. In a similar way, for the appropriate teachers to gain benefit from a discussion of this class's reputation, a credible facilitator who can organise detailed discussion is needed, although this discussion would not in the first instance take place in the same context as the pupil's. The most important element is that the person leading the discussion has the belief that reputations can be altered, so that the discussion will generate pointers for action, and does not adopt a fixed or passive view towards these social processes. On some occasions where a class reputation has not been modified, this crucial element has been missing. In more general terms, it seems useful to recognise that the open investigation, discussion, and influence of reputations will not generate change if the allocation of reputations is linked to a central feature of the school as an organisation, which would not be primarily addressed in this approach. Examples include attempts to influence the reputation of 'the dumb class' in a school which is tightly streamed and which chooses to value inter-group competition: here the discussion approach may serve merely to express the anger and resentment which may exist. Such examples serve as reminders that interventions at the whole-class level depend on the possibility for change at the whole-school level, as discussed in the previous chapter.

At this point is seems worthwhile to remember that this section has analysed a rare event; whole-class disruption. The reasons were argued earlier and were developed from the recognition that classrooms are complex and multidimensional. In most secondary schools there exists another reason why whole-class disruption is rare – it is that, especially in the later years, whole classes do not spend significant amounts of their time together, since they are separated and re-arranged by setting and option practices. Rather than being able to view the class as a stable peer group, it is more appropriate to conceptualise the situation as a series of changing 'interaction sets' (Furlong, 1976). By this phrase we mean to highlight that pupils, even when they are in the same class, will be behaving towards different groups of pupils for the different events which occur, and that such groupings are fluid and changing according to the event. 'The interaction set at any one time will be those pupils who perceive what is happening in a similar way, communicate this to each other and define appropriate action together.' Carol interacts with her two mates in mind for some things, but with the whole class on others, and so on. Here it is possible to see that although interaction sets are generally changing, the examples of whole-class disruption examined above are exactly the occasions when the interation set is fixed and includes the whole class – the whole class then acts together, with the whole class in mind, towards the teacher. This is uncommon, and even more uncommon is the occasion when a class acts towards a number of teachers (ie the school) in this way. Setting practices and options arrangements reduce this likelihood.

Viewing classes as 'interaction sets' takes us on from the rare whole-class disruption to consider the more frequently occurring examples of part-class disruption. As was suggested earlier, this is often the state of affairs in what feels to the teacher to be whole-class disruption. It is on these occasions that we properly move to analyse the role being played by various pupils in their various sub-groups. What notions are available to aid our analysis? What useful tools can our enquiry employ? What possible interventions follow?

Part-class disruption

When a sub-group of pupils is causing a teacher difficulty, and examination suggests that the problem is not reflecting organisational or whole-class issues, the understandable reaction is often that of focusing on particular members of the group and attempting to intervene through these individuals. Talk of ringleaders and the like is a highlighted example. However, the most visible members of a group are not necessarily the sources of power and influence in that group. Indeed, to locate the power of a group in any individual leads to an impoverished view. At this point we need to take seriously the notion of roles in groups.

The term role is not intended to signify a formal position with a set of duties (for example, the role of mayor) but rather a cluster of behaviours which is meaningful to others (for example the role of class clown). This could be described as informal role.

An important point follows immediately. The behaviours which we make sense of under any role title are not necessarily the full repertoire of behaviours of that person. For example, if we understand some of a pupil's behaviour and refer to it as being the class clown, we have not described all of that pupil's behaviour. To believe that we had would confuse an informal role title with the less useful notion of a personality label. Everyday examples help us keep this point in mind. The fact that a man is a father and can be seen to exercise that role towards his children does not mean we have a total description: he will (like everyone else) enact a number of roles, each in their respective context. It is possible to avoid the trap of equating informal role titles with over-simple or all-embracing labels for people.

A second fundamental point about role is that any role is enacted towards particular other people and can be enacted only when those others, termed the role partners, play their part in the interaction. A leader cannot be a leader without followers, the bully cannot be a bully without victims. It becomes important to view roles in connection with their role partners in order to obtain a sufficiently full picture. It may be more correct to say that we use the term role to describe one actor's contribution to a meaningful set of transactions. Anyone who has attempted to enact a role (even that of teacher) in a context where the others are not responding in a way which validates and recognises that enactment will have experienced the power of this point, alongside the experience of their attempt collapsing!

When analysing the behaviour of pupil groups in classroom it therefore follows that rather than focusing on supposedly problematic individuals, we will create a more powerful picture by looking at how the various roles relate and interact in the playing out of the behaviour in that group. (If it seems to transpire that one person's contribution does not much depend on the role of others then a group role analysis is possibly inappropriate, and the methods of the next chapter will prove useful).

One final orienting point is worthwhile. If pupils do not spend all their time in the same grouping but find themselves in a range of interaction sets, it follows that the roles they portray will not be the same. This may be fairly obvious when taken across obviously differing contexts such as home, school and neighbourhood, but is also worthy of consideration by schools across situations which are more apparently similar, such as the range of classes a pupil meets.

Having made these introductory points about role, we now face another tricky aspect: how to describe in a methodical way roles in groups. Everyday terms for the stances people adopt in groups will not suffice as they are not necessarily based on any systematic view and therefore are unlikely to contribute any systematic benefits to our thinking. This may be particularly the case in classrooms where, as writers such as Hargreaves (1975, p 235) have argued, the teacher is liable to conceptualise informal group functioning entirely from her/his perspective. But systems for describing group roles are not easy to find: even the most relevant texts (Schmuck and Schmuck, 1979; Hargreaves, 1975) do not provide answers. We have found the work of Bales (1970) most useful and will now present a distillation of his findings: we hope he would not be too distressed at the presentation of hundreds of pages of his text in a simplified diagram!

Bales' research on group functioning found that the roles people adopted in groups could be described along three important dimensions. The first captured the degree to which the person exercised power or dominance in the group: one's position could be upward or downward on this dimension. The second illustrates the degree of liking or the evaluation a person attracts: one's position could be positive or negative on this dimension. The third portrays the degree of contribution to the group tasks: a person may be forward or backward on this dimension. Thus, we have a three-dimensional 'social evaluative space' into which it is possible to locate the general role style of group members (Figure 3.1).

This conceptual framework can be of direct use as it stands. With practice it is soon possible to array the various members of a group in the space by deciding their position on the three dimensions. This task

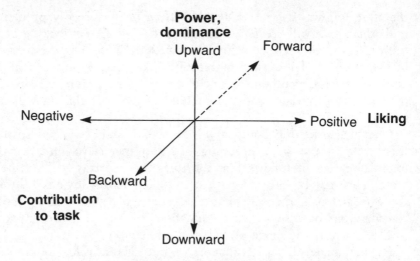

Figure 3.1   The three dimensions of social evaluation (Bales, 1970)

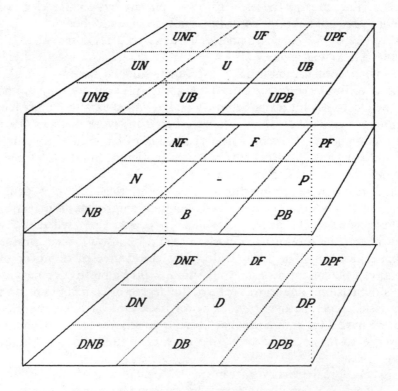

Figure 3.2   Bales' 26 'role types' and their positional abbreviations

can be facilitated by reference to Bales' twenty-six 'role types' which are generated by allowing three major positions on each of the three dimensions. Figure 3.2 shows these in diagrammatic form (with their positional abbreviations which show the various combinations of Upward-Downward, Positive-Negative, and Backward-Forward. Thus DPF would denote Downward, Positive, Forward).

However, it seems unlikely that the pastoral team will create direct benefit with colleagues from this system as it stands. Imagine walking into the staffroom and asking a colleague whether they thought John Jones was a DP or a PB!

We present in Figure 3.3 our own attempt to fit everyday descriptive words to the Bales framework so that a systematic description of group roles may develop.

For example, to the 'role type' PB, which stands for Positive on liking, Backward on contribution to the task, and neutral on the exercise of power, we give the description 'socialiser'. And the 'role

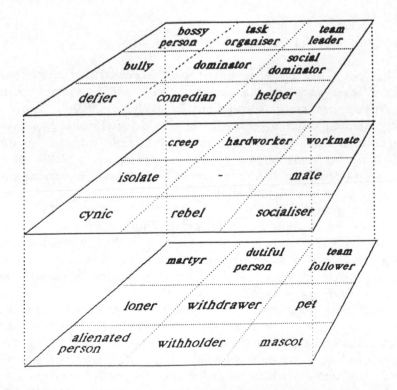

Figure 3.3 Possible short descriptions for the Bales framework of 'role types'

type' UPF, which stands for Upward on the exercise of power, Positive on liking, and Forward on contribution to the task, can be seen as a popular 'team leader'.

This model and its role descriptions can help us:
i have a more differentiated view of the roles which may operate in a group, together with a sense of the dimensions along which they differ,
ii recognise some of the interconnections between roles and their role-partners (for example the bully and the victims),
iii understand some of the occasions when people in some roles do not get on smoothly (for example, Bales suggests that many of the 'upward' types will argue with the type listed diametrically opposite to them on that level, and similarly for the types who are 'downward'),
iv provide a more systematic framework with which to analyse a small group which is generating difficulties in a classroom.

Surveying pupil roles in classroom groups

At this point we will again put forward a powerful strategy for the pastoral team when (on this occasion) faced with an example of less-than-whole-class group disruption. It involves gathering systematic information in order to create a suitably detailed picture of events. Rather than react by focusing on highly visible members, a quick collection of information will provide a more dynamic picture of how the group operates and thus suggest some further interventions whose effect could be more long lasting.

Given a group of pupils who engage the attention of the pastoral team, the information likely to prove illuminating concerns i the membership and boundaries of the group, and ii the role relationships in the group, across a range of situations. In the secondary school the separate subject lessons can act as a convenient definer of the situations, as in the following example:

A particular group of five fourth-year girls have been brought to the head of year's attention particularly by the English teacher. In the English lessons, which are taught in tutor groups, the five girls form a distinct and quite strongly coherent group which spends much of its energy on topics other than the tasks set by the English teacher. Two of the girls have occasional confrontations, so the overall effect is to ignore or disrupt the teachers' intentions.

The head of year knows each of the girls and among the five are a fair proportion of 'strong characters' – quite assertive, talkative and often in the teacher's attention.

Information has been collected from three other teachers, who have been asked to describe the girls' roles according to the above system, trying to make sure that the perspective they adopt to describe is that of the girls' group rather than that of the teacher. By this we mean that the teachers are asked to give a description of the girls' roles as they operate from the point of view of the girls' group, and thus utilise the girls' judgments about liking, influence, and so on. This contrasts with a description given from the teacher's point of view as manager of the whole classroom, and thus does not intend to contain the teachers' judgments about liking, influence and so on from her/his point of view. A model form for this exercise is given in Figure 3.5 at the end of this section (p 85). The results are shown in Figure 3.4 below, together with some of the additional observations.

Maths lessons are in ability sets and the teacher reports a not very strong group with the presence of Anne from another tutor group, and Anne's more aggressive qualities. In the humanities lesson the group is without Mary (in a pure history class) and Anne (in a local studies class), and the atmosphere is reported as congenial, with Linda adopting a more dominating position. In the biology class all six girls are present and a strong working atmosphere has been generated, to the extent that Anne's attempts to be bossy are generally unsuccessful (the teacher had added the qualification 'tries to be' to the description) with the very occasional exception of annoying Linda.

How can this information help us decide on effective intervention, especially toward the situation in English lessons? From the English

Figure 3.4

	English	Maths	Humanities	Biology
Anita	defier	—	comedian	comedian
Mary	team leader	team leader	—	hard worker
Linda	socialiser	social dominator	social dominator	socialiser
Dawn	mate	—	mate	workmate
Paula	socialiser	team follower	team follower	team follower
Anne	—	bully	—	bossy

teacher's view an approach could be to get Anita to exercise more self-control and exhort the whole group to more work. But this would ignore the fact that Anita has self-control (and that general exhortations to work are often impotent).

Is there another individual on which to focus an intervention? To many teachers Mary would present herself as a candidate for consideration at this point since she is seen as leader: get her to be more as she is in biology and perhaps the rest would follow? This strategy contains a major pitfall – in suggesting to Mary that she changes from team leader to hard worker in the English lessons, we would implicitly be asking her to relinquish her leader position: this would have little chance of success. On many occasions leaders have less room for manoeuvre in their behaviour than do other members of the group: they must maintain the conduct of the group sometimes in the face of leadership challenges. In this example we would be asking Mary to give up both status and liking by others (and we would be assuming without evidence that Mary was the motive force in generating the atmosphere prevailing in biology).

Another possible candidate for some of the more social leadership functions is Linda. However, at first sight there is not much benefit to be clearly gained from Linda being socially more dominant while Mary and Anita are present. But at least Linda and Anita do not compete for dominance, so it may be possible that Linda could be powerful here, by encouraging Anita's comedian rather than defier role.

Here we have seen an example of considering one person for their effects on others in the group. A further example could focus on Dawn. She has a more task-oriented role in the more productive atmosphere of the biology class and it would be unwise to assume that she had no role in helping to create that atmosphere. It would be possible to encourage her to be more work-oriented in English, especially if this was in coalition with Mary.

The above example has utilised two important notions. *Considering a small group and focusing on individuals who could become appropriate change agents:*

a choose someone who has sufficient room for manoeuvre in their conduct, and

b take an indirect approach by choosing someone who as change agent will have an effect on the individuals you first identified as a cause for concern.

Having considered one approach to small-group disruption and its link to teacher intervention of an indirect style towards individuals in the group, it may be a short step to consider teacher intervention towards pairs of group members or even the whole group. The example above no doubt led many readers to the view that some part of the situation in English may have been changed by engaging Anita and Mary in an analysis of their occasional confrontations. The aim would be to encourage them to extend their understanding of how their roles related and to find their own way of achieving more satisfying interactions for both of them. This can be seen as a fairly direct approach to the pair: its success depends on their wishing to change the pattern of interaction: there are occasions where approaches as direct as this will not succeed, as the following example suggests.

Babatunde and Michael are in the second year and they are continually being referred to the year head for disruptive episodes in lessons. They engage in 'cussing' each other: this involves exchanging personal insults in a gradually escalating manner, leading up to remarks about their respective mothers, at which point a scuffle breaks out. Teachers have tried various approaches: separating them leads to calling out across the classroom, detentions are attended happily (once their mothers have been informed) and sometimes provide an arena for more cussing. The head of year is almost at a loss to know what to try. However, the form tutor knows that Babatunde and Michael spend much of their out-of-school time together, and also notes that when the two are being carpeted for their disruption they show no resentment toward each other.

It seems possible that rather than being aggresive enemies, these two are in fact quite close, but their style of interacting does not immediately convey this to outsiders. On reflection the cussing itself is personal, shows they know each other, is predictable in its escalation, allows physical testing-out, and leads to some extra variety in the school situations they have to cope with together – it has features of a strong coalition: even the school's response has served to confirm this coalition on the basis of their disruptiveness. The tutors now see how their sensible professional attempts to persuade Babatunde and Michael to give up the cussing is tantamount to asking them to give up showing that they are friends. Here, therefore, an indirect approach is called for, one in which the closeness between the two is not challenged but the disruptive version is not inadvertently maintained by the school's approach.

Teachers developed the strategy of giving the duo joint tasks on which they cooperated in lessons and, if any outbreaks of cussing occurred, just one of them would be sent to the head of department, who would find an alternative place to work. Note that this strategy is clearly linked to the understanding which has developed of their behaviour. It values their friendship in its productive aspects, and intervenes only to separate them when things become disruptive. It is more creative than the gross strategy which some might suggest of separating Michael and Babatunde permanently, with a risk of attracting their resentment and a poorer performance in learning.

The final consideration in this section on part-class disruption raises another style of intervention, that of working with the whole group of pupils whose effect is disruptive. We hestitate to use the term 'group counselling' for this work, not because it is an inaccurate term to apply, but because there are so many unfortunate connotations and misunderstandings attached to the notion of counselling. Here we indicate a process of working with a group of pupils which involves structured discussions aimed at *i* eliciting and respecting their views of each other and of the processes they are involved in, *ii* extending the understandings which are being used and opening up the discussion of whether changes are likely to bring benefits – this can involve some teaching and does not involve collusion, *iii* generating and evaluating strategies for change together with issues in their implementation. A number of meetings will be required for this work, and the staff member undertaking it will require credibility and skill – considerations similar to those on p 74 may apply. Further discussion of group counselling may be found in Hamblin (1974).

The group process is unlikely to be effective in changing patterns which generate disruption if the central phase fails, that is, the group's extended understanding and discussion of its own functioning does not identify any dissatisfactions its members have and which help to form the agenda for change. This can arise on two main types of occasion. The first is when a group of pupils is well aware of its disruptive effect, accepts its responsibility for the effect and is well aware of the responses the school is likely to make. Yet still there is no wish to make change, probably because the experience of testing boundaries and creating excitement is more rewarding than the alternatives which the school suggests. On these occasions our attention is drawn back once again to the school's curriculum and its climate for young people. The second is when a group of pupils does not consider itself responsible for the disruptive effects and locates the cause in some other specific source, such as an individual subject or teacher. If this is backed up by the survey or teachers, our attention is drawn on to working with the teacher, the focus of the remainder of this chapter. Both these examples serve as timely reminders that there is no power to control others' agendas associated with the adoption of counselling approaches, and that 'counselling disruptives' can be a spurious notion unless the pupils whose effect is disruptive are also pupils who want change. Group counselling can be relevant for the general theme under discussion here; changing group roles and the implied communication within the group. This is the focal theme which may be attached to a variety of starting points (indeed, the group of girls being thought about in the example above seemed to show some change of classroom behaviour after group work on an apparently unrelated matter – drug abuse – amongst a wider group).

Surveying Pupils' Roles

To: .... From:.

This form has been designed to help in gaining a full picture of how a particular group of pupils operates and what roles these pupils take up in the group (and class group) in which they are members. The form will be circulated to all colleagues whose lessons include most or all of the pupils, and will then be used to construct a composite picture for discussion.

Pupils who cause concern: ....
....
....
....
....
....

Please adopt the following format:

1. Against each pupil name above write the role name from the list attached which you consider most nearly describes that pupil's behaviour in the group. These descriptions are from the perspective of the group itself, rather than the whole class.
2. If in your lesson other pupils seem to be significant members of the group, please add them to the list together with the appropriate role name.
3. Please add any additional comments you think could be helpful in increasing our understanding.

This is meant to take only a few minutes reflection. Could you please return it to me in the next few days?

Many thanks

Date   /   /

Figure 3.5 A model form for use in role survey continued over

List of group role names:
(as applying in this group context)

	(additional description)
Team leader	helps progress, sociable, conscientious
Workmate	agreeable, responsible, caring
Team follower	friendly, submissive, gentle
Task organiser	gives suggestions, encourages loyalty
Hard worker	instrumental, conservative
Dutiful person	hardworking, conventional, impersonal
Bossy person	dominates, unfriendly
Creep	attracts dislike, highly conscientious
Martyr	self-sacrificing, attracts aggression
Social dominator	confident, extroverted
Mate	friendly, sociable, an equal
Pet	friendly, trusting, imitator
Dominator	talkative, self-confident
Withdrawer	self-effacing, seems powerless
Bully	dominant, aggressive
Isolate	disliked, solitary
Loner	unresponsive, unfriendly, rejecting
Helper	expressive, open, friendly
Socialiser	likeable, responsive, companionable
Mascot	friendly, non-assertive, passive
Comedian	expressive, jokey
Rebel	rejects group beliefs
Withholder	tense, unco-operative, passive
Defier	dominating, self-centred, rebellious
Cynic	unfriendly, obstinate, anti-conformist
Alienated person	unfriendly, dejected, disillusioned

Classroom management issues

When the pastoral team is engaged in school discipline issues, no amount of analysis of school ethos and curriculum or pupil group dynamics or individual pupil characteristics will allow them to escape what is on some occasions an inescapable conclusion – the teacher is a major element in the classroom situation and can be creating conditions which generate difficulties. We all know this, so why is it worth stating? Mainly because there are tendencies in schools and teachers which serve to avoid focusing the cause for difficulties on the classroom teacher. Many of these tendencies are positive: they seek to avoid processes of blaming, scapegoating or generally attributing excessive responsibility to an individual teacher. But some are not so positive in their effects: they perhaps reflect the culture of teaching and its role strain (see p 67) where a protective individualism grows up, masked by the notion of 'autonomy', serving to hide the fears of evalution in a profession where performance is very difficult to judge. (Hargreaves, 1982). Certainly it becomes rare to find examples of teachers who, when faced with classroom difficulties, attribute much cause to themselves and ask 'What have I got wrong that has created this?'

Given this context, what is the pastoral care team to do to help an individual teacher? The view of this book, reflected in the theoretical and practical approach, is that much can be achieved. It will not be achieved if we locate the cause for difficulty in some fixed personal quality such as teacher 'personality' – that would also be unacceptable on the grounds that a teacher's behaviour is a function of person and situation. Further, not much will be achieved if the pastoral team really believes that the teacher is to blame in some simple fashion. Instead, keeping in mind the extent to which the teacher is one element in a complex situation will assist us in adopting a suitably complex view and consequently seeing new possibilities for change.

This section examines the ways in which help can be offered, while avoiding the traps of judgment and blame. Without this aspect as part of the overall approach the pastoral team's work is unethical. The two main themes to be raised are: *i* changing the teacher's effect on the classroom situation; *ii* changing the patterns of particular interactions.

We start with the reminder that the highly visible aspects of a teacher's performance may not be the most powerful factors affecting the classroom, and the recognition that focusing on the teacher's obvious actions from the outset is not likely to create a climate which leads to the teacher making changes, especially if things have already become emotionally charged.

Change in the teacher's effect in the classroom situation can come in a number of ways, involving the physical, social and psychological aspects of the setting, together with how these relate together in the teacher's planning of activities.

The physical aspects of many secondary school classrooms have improved in one dimension over the past decade – their colourfulness and attractiveness. However, recent years have also seen a decline in the state of repair. Against this background it is important to draw attention to the fact that teachers often do not impose themselves on the physical aspect. Partly this is because the typical approach to school timetabling results in teachers being moved around a number of classrooms not of their choice – little wonder that the study by Corrie *et al* (1982) found that teachers do not feel in charge of their working environments. Yet on occasions when teachers have a firm base their classroom management is enhanced: the signs of 'ownership' and the social messages conveyed through the selection of objects and layout all serve to indicate that one person is in charge of the territory to a degree. On occasions of giving assistance to teachers experiencing difficulty it is not unusual to see them conveying the message that they have little control or ownership of the situation's physical features, let alone other aspects. On some of these occasions it can be an effective place to start discussion, since it is potentially powerful and at the same time non-threatening to the teacher.

Considerations of display, colour, and even lighting can lead to easy changes which affect pupil behaviour. The final step to anticipate is that of ensuring the change is a positive one. Pupil response to new stimuli may provide a short-term respite for the teacher in a positive way, but keeping the effect up will need more than novelty. As an aside it may be worth anticipating the response by other members of staff – there are occasionally deep-seated views which associate colour and care for environment with frivolity and junior age ranges, and sometimes even with a particular gender.

Consideration of classroom layout brings dividends. At the most basic level some classrooms are organised so as to create traffic 'hot spots', which in turn generate unwelcome behaviour. At a more significant level perhaps the layout of furniture and the arrangement of seating carries a number of potential messages about expectations of work patterns, who is to be attended to, who work partners are, to indicate what sort of learner the pupil is expected to be. The standard lines of desks convey different messages from those conveyed by paired desks, or grouped tables with six chairs. The messages conveyed concern the activity level which is expected of pupils, the amount of interaction which is expected between them, the types of tasks they will tackle and, by implication, who is to be responsible for the learning. Two facing banks of desks on either side of a room could create unwelcome effects. Could we imagine a classroom with two concentric circles of desks? And for each of these patterns we may consider their effect on behaviour and on learners' views of themselves, especially the degree to which they are seen as responsible by teachers.

These features are often not used to good effect by the teacher experiencing difficulty. There may have been a move to a fixed strategy of the rows of desks layout in the face of difficulty, but paradoxically this may bring exactly the opposite result to that intended, through the focusing of even more attention on the teacher. That extra attention may not in fact enhance teacher control because too much emphasis is being given to the teacher's direct control attempts, and all the other means through which s/he may exert influence are forgotten. These other means interrelate to a strong degree. Seating layouts need considering alongside seating plans and alongside that central feature, the activities that have been planned.

Seating plans are an example of how the physical setting and the social structure of classrooms interrelate, yet again they are an example of how teachers sometimes do not influence the environment in which they work. Sometimes the arguments one hears between proponents of a particular criterion for arranging pupils, or between any of those proponents and the advocates of free choice, seem to be bound to end in disagreement. So it remains the case that teachers' organisation of pupils' seating positions is associated in pupils' and teachers' minds with punishment and/or excessive control. There is a considerable need for more practice in explaining to pupils the good reasons for organising seating, and the important positive learnings which can follow. In the meantime, work with colleagues on this aspect of classrooms can be fruitful, even though attention must be given to the rate at which change is attempted: wholesale rearrangements are less likely to be taken up (or even attempted) much after the beginning of the school year and the creation of a history to the classroom interactions.

Consideration of the psychological aspects of the situation encompasses many of the features we have discussed in an earlier section (pp 66–69). These include the timing, pacing and routines of the classroom, together with the group focus and involvement of pupils in effective activities. These are centrally important elements in the creation of a purposeful classroom climate and can be discussed in a manner which is not perceived as threatening or personally judgmental to the teacher in difficulty – they refer to the teacher as situation manager rather than to the teacher in a more personally involving way.

With practice each element can be observed and its function discussed with a fellow teacher (it may be effective to start with an analyis of one's own lessons first, and then those of some friendly colleagues). The following focusing questions help.

Timing of activities
- Is the time allowed for the next step communicated clearly in advance?

- Is the timing of steps long enough not to cause pupil frustration, and short enough not to lose pupil attention or cause dissatisfaction?
- Can the times allowed be renegotiated?

Pacing of activities

- Is the number of activities in the lesson adequate? (Many teachers plan for only one activity per lesson.)
- Is changeover between activities handled clearly and pace maintained?
- Is the pace appropriate for the intended learning?

Group focus of activities

- Is the class divided up into groups quickly and smoothly?
- Are the sizes of groups clearly stated and changes of group size incorporated in the lesson?
- Is the composition of groups controlled and explained?

Pupil involvement in activities

- Are the goals and demands of the tasks clearly communicated?
- Is opportunity for talk included? Does the task engage the pupils in problem-solving and appraisal of solutions?
- Is the need for pupil collaboration clearly communicated, built into the task and the assessment?

The above elements are of significance in the central skill of planning activities, and of sustaining pupil cooperation with the activities. At the same time their successful management can give rise to a purposeful classroom climate with clear structures and boundaries. It is on these elements that classroom order is built rather than on the teacher's personal style. Classroom order is vested in the activities, not in the person of the teacher. This can be a difficult learning to accommodate for the teacher in difficulty: s/he may have adopted a belief that extended control is achieved by extended personal influence of a direct sort (more than a few superficially successful teachers adopt this belief too). It may take a little time to persuade a colleague to experiment on one of these non-obvious elements of classroom life, but the end result will have the benefit not only of bringing attention to the powerful influence of these elements, but also of temporarily reducing the attention given to features of the teacher's performance.

The teacher's interaction with pupils in the classoom is the second theme of this section, particularly changing the patterns of particular interactions. Again the approach will need to take care not to become involved in simple blaming processes, or in negative personal criticism, but should identify clear features of the teacher's part in interaction which would profit from modification. And again, this approach is more likely to be achieved by remembering that teacher behaviour *prior* to student misbehaviour is most likely to be influential, and by recognising that these issues in interaction face every teacher. In this way we shall avoid dividing teachers into the two spurious camps of effective and ineffective.

At the most global level it is fruitful to investigate how a teacher establishes her/himself in the classroom, and how s/he projects the 'definition of the situation' which s/he intends will prevail. This term is not intended to connote a fixed set of definitions about the classroom, but is intended to convey a collection of interconnected meanings about the interaction in the classroom: the teacher's role, her/his goals, the students' roles, their goals, what each thinks of the other, the emergent definition of how teaching and learning are conducted and their relation to other aspects of classroom behaviour. Should the teacher fail to convey her/his definition of the situation in a convincing manner, it is likely s/he will perceive much of the pupil behaviour as deviant, not because the pupil's definition of the situation necessarily conflicts or clashes with the teacher's but because the two will rarely coincide without persuasion and influence from the teacher. This influence on the part of the teacher is unlikely to be successful if it depends on imposition alone: deference cannot be expected, and a variety of negotiations will take place before a working consensus is achieved.

Note that up to this point nothing has been said about the *content* of the teacher's definition of the situation, the actual beliefs and meanings that the teacher adopts. Nor is it likely that any attempt to specify such content for successful teaching would be meaningful. There is considerable diversity across teachers, across the subjects, pupils, ages they teach and so on. This point has a similar impact to that common statement 'there are as many successful teaching styles as successful teachers' (and the converse). It reminds us not to look for the explanatory features at an inappropriate level of analysis.

If we cannot be prescriptive about the content of the teacher's definition, can we usefully say anything about the way in which the working consensus is approached? Certainly there seem to be crucially differing outcomes possible in resolving the differing perspectives. Hargreaves' (1975) terms of concord, discord, and pseudo-concord are evocative.

The issue here is probably best described under the term 'negotiation', but there are some connotations of that term which need to be mentioned and excluded. Negotiation is not intended to mean a process of protracted talk about every minor aspect: that focuses too much on the verbal. Nor does it mean a process of horse-trading or bargaining. Negotiating a view of a classroom is intended to describe a complex process of giving meaning to events, conveying those meanings in one's interactions, perhaps modifying them in the light of experience, and perhaps experimenting with them on occasions. It is important to note that we are not using the term to suggest that negotiations between teacher and pupil in a classroom are 'status equal' transactions; indeed researchers such as Martin (1975) have suggested that 75% of teacher–pupil negotiations end with the teacher's view prevailing. Thus the difference in formal power is reflected in interactions. Our use of the term negotiation is not intended to suggest that all aspects of classroom interaction will be open to revision: the formal roles ascribed, the personal identities of the participants are generally not negotiable.

However, within these delimitations of the term we may now attempt to iluminate the complexity of any particular teacher's negotation of her/his definition of the classroom situation under the following interconnected headings:

- classroom climate
- teachers' strategies
- teachers' communication
- associated aspects of teachers' thinking
- teachers' self-presentation.

The notion of classroom climate can on occasion be rather 'slippery' for those attempting an empirical measurement of the notion. But the comment by Fox *et al* (1966) still seems difficult to challenge: 'Both experience and research show that pupils tend to respond favourably to the learning situation when the teacher presents his/her methods and objectives to them clearly and concretely, when s/he makes frequent checks of their reactions to classroom activities, and when s/he takes their points of view into consideration.' We are aiming to generate a climate which is clear, purposeful, rewarding, responsive and engaging. There is no single method of achieving this which will apply in all contexts, but the teacher's style of communication and negotiation will be a major element, as detailed below.

Teacher's strategies when faced with things not going so smoothly are another important facet of their style in negotiating their definition of the situation. The speed with which some potential conflicts can escalate into confrontations is surprising to some teachers and these processes need to be analysed in detail. Clarke's (1981) detailed analysis of the internal structure of disruptive incidents demonstrated that 'soft' and discursive strategies were much more likely to lead to an exit from the incident than were hard commands. There is therefore, research backing for a non-confronting strategy. Pik's (1981) suggestions on preventing and handling confrontations are useful, and the insights into teachers' depth of feeling are illuminating, but in some ways divert attention from the focus for this section – teachers' strategies for de-escalating conflicts. Reynolds (1976) has suggested that when teachers and pupils refuse a truce this is an indicator of extended difficulty within a school. There seems to be ample evidence in favour of a clear focus on de-escalation and preventing confrontations, and on examining and teaching these processes through staff workshops.

On the occasions when a confrontation of some kind appears to be developing, the following principles seem to encourage de-escalation:

- Avoid public arenas in which people may crystallise their position in front of an audience.
- Ask 'Is what has led to this really so important as to justify this escalation?'
- Avoid threats of any sort, especially those which could be perceived as physical.
- Look for an alternative which is presently not being explored in which *both* can 'win'.
- Encourage the pupil to say more about his/her perception of what is going on.
- Explain your own view of things clearly, and in a way which is not simplified.

With practice these principles can be applied in such a way that teachers' common reactions about feelings of 'condoning' or 'climbing down' are not precipitated, and teachers can agree that desired behaviour from pupils is not brought about by confrontation.

Further specific features may be identified through a focus on the teachers' communication in classroom interaction. Communication about the rules and routines which a teacher intends to establish has always been a major element in interactionist views of classrooms (eg Hargreaves, 1975; Hargreaves *et al*, 1975), and yet many classrooms contain little talk on this topic, not always because the rules and routines have become agreed and workable. Clear statements of rules being invoked and their rationales are an important aspect of the teacher's repertoire, not because rule-following will immediately occur, by any stretch of the imagination, but because they are an aspect of the teacher making a claim for his/her own definition of the classroom. They are an initial stance in an important negotiation and as such can contribute to the sense of purpose in the situation. Associated with rationales for rules are rationales for the classroom activities, but these are in surprisingly short supply in some classrooms. Practice in finding one's own response to the pupil's question 'What's the point of this?' can lead to improved presentation of classroom activity and enhanced feelings of responsibility by the teacher. This process is probably of heightened importance at the present time, when old rationales for the long-term benefits of education seem less powerful and teachers are having to find new rationales for adolescents who believe that school offers less to their future lives. This discussion of rationales is not meant to imply that teachers and classrooms are or should be understood as rational: rather it implies that the rationales and justifications a teacher gives are an important aspect of their negotiation repertoire.

Communication about rules is also of significance when the teacher is changing the activity in a classroom, and thus the rules for interaction in the classroom. Hargreaves *et al* (1975) observed classroom rules and grouped them into five themes – talk, movement, time, teacher–pupil relations, and pupil–pupil relations – noticing that the different phases of a lesson had different combinations of rules 'in play'. But how then are rules or their combinations changed to create the different phases and sub-phases? And does it make a difference how these changes are handled? Kounin (1970) found that the teacher's success at communicating a change of rule structure was strongly connected with the amount of deviance which followed, in that, if the change was unsuccessfully communicated, not only would pupils be engaged in a wider ranger of actions but also the teacher would be perceiving many of these actions as contrary to the new rule set. Thus, practice in 'switch signals' (and their usual preface of an attention-getter) such as 'Right, now it's time to turn our attention to . . .' can have positive effects.

Not very far detached from any teacher's style of communicating in classrooms lies their style of thinking about classroom events and interactions. Although this is not, of course, observable in the classroom, any support work for teachers experiencing difficulty will soon be faced with examples of how teachers think and especially of how they think about pupil behaviour which disrupts the teacher's intentions. Of particular importance here is the way in which a teacher may attribute cause and motive for a particular pupil behaviour. Lawrence, Steed and Young (1983) have researched the factors which lead teachers to view some instances of misbehaviour as serious: these are *a* where the teacher perceives the incident as the latest in a series, *b* where the teacher thinks that the pupil is 'getting at' him/her personally and the behaviour is seen as intentional, malicious, and *c* where there is some extra pressure acting on the teacher. Teachers vary in the degree to which they perceive behaviours in the above terms, which is the very reason why these processes may be discussed with profit: those who are experiencing difficulty and who attribute serious deviance quickly can learn from their colleagues who are less likely to adopt such perceptions and whose repertoire for negotiation extends accordingly. In this we are perhaps accepting the work of Martin (1975), who suggested that teachers attribute to their pupils differing degrees of negotiability, and classify pupils into negotiable/intermittently negotiable/non-negotiable. But in accepting this idea we would also be wanting to accept that the aim of the pastoral team is to reduce the number of pupils who are classified in the third category.

Finally, and at a more global level, it may be important to examine the more impressionistic features of a teacher's performance, when help is being offered. One part of what teachers are negotiating in their classroom can be described as their self-presentation. By this term we mean the manner and style in which teachers present themselves and which pupils take note of. Gannaway's (1976) research suggested that fourth-year pupils evaluated a teacher's performance on two important aspects of self-presentation through the questions 'Can he have a laugh?' and 'Does he understand pupils?'. Perhaps both of these are elements in how pupils may come to regard a classroom as having a responsive climate. Certainly they highlight how a presentation which focuses completely on task features of classroom life will be disengaging for pupils. Yet this can often be a feature of teachers' self-presentation in a classroom with difficulties – an apparent belief that the only focus for both teacher and pupils must be the task at hand, with a strong exclusion of passing 'engagements' with other topics. The climate thus generated can take on the quality of an ongoing battle in which the teacher may end up with a beleaguered rather than triumphant look.

Workshops on classroom management

Classrooms are complex places and in some ways they are becoming more complex. At a time when teachers are having to re-assess the rationales they offer, there is also an increased impetus towards cooperative and collaborative learning for pupils and an added emphasis on the use of activity-based learning methods. These developments do not necessarily make classroom management more difficult, but they do make classroom management something different from what many colleagues have exercised in the past.

There is a considerable need for teachers to review and sometimes restructure their classroom practice. As one aspect of the pastoral care of staff, the pastoral team should be sensitively aware of this need for staff development, especially as it will affect all staff, not only the ones who experience difficulties as considered in this chapter. As resources and expertise in school-based staff development increase, one aspect of the pastoral task is to identify, vocalise and with others to offer assistance towards the needs for considering classroom management. Some colleagues with pastoral care responsibilities may feel it is 'risky' for them to bring attention to such a central feature of all teachers' work, but it is much more risky in the long term if no one addresses the issue.

Workshops for staff must give due attention to the climate in which they are held, especially the sensitivity of teachers to making public their teaching performance. Voluntary group meetings which develop alongside the development of collaborative teaching in classrooms will perhaps be profitable, and as with all change attempts a lengthy timescale should be anticipated.

A strategy is required which builds on strengths, helps colleagues talk about their present successes and consider what works for them. Approaches to change must be gradual and cumulative, building on the gains which have emanated from early small changes. The form of talk in discussions is likely to avoid unhelpful notions such as 'teacher personality' or the over-simple views of 'teacher's style', if these are viewed as relatively unchangeable. Rather, the discussion will focus on concrete and specific skills and practices, providing the sort of detailed talk between colleagues which is lacking in many teachers' professional experience.

The exact topics for workshop meetings need to be negotiated with those attending, perhaps by asking for responses to a list of topics, such as:

- making sense of the classroom situation (cf p 63)
- managing the classroom setting (cf p 70)
- planning activities in a lesson (cf p 71)
- understanding pupil roles (cf p 76)
- classroom rules and routines (cf p 89)
- classroom climate (cf p 92)
- teacher strategies and negotiation including 'de-escalating' (cf p 93)
- teacher communication, including 'switch signals' (cf p 94)
- (add others)

The use of the term 'workshop' is deliberate here since the meetings will need to have an active approach through the use of case studies, discussion activities, role play and so on. Videos can be made in school, others are available commercially (Amphlett, 1985). Setting up monitoring tasks or experiments for the period between meetings will stimulate transfer of the issues from the workshop sessions, and will encourage a style of realistic investigation rather than excessive introspection. The sharing of the variety of perspectives which members of a group bring is powerful in the generation of new strategies, and also helps move the workshop leader's role away from that of 'the source of good practice'. Groups which create a process of the supposedly skilled talking to the supposedly unskilled are unlikely to generate real change.

Perhaps some of the suggestions for discussion and investigation given at the end of this chapter may be profitably modified for use in these workshops. They have the intended function of focusing attention in a structured and actively investigative way on identifiable features of classroom life. They may help to generate the sort of atmosphere which is most productive in such workshops: an atmosphere which is active, investigative and experimental rather than one which becomes over-individualised and personalised in its focus. When teacher colleagues want change to occur it is wanted in their classrooms: thus, any workshop which seems to carry the over-personalising message of 'come to these meetings and change yourself so that your classrooms change' will probably lose its capacity to engage colleagues.

Similar points will apply in the next chapter when we examine strategies for making sense of individuals in classrooms. There again we shall see that over-individualising the issues can prevent change. As in this chapter and in this book as a whole, the order in which things are examined is crucial, and the examination of context first leads to greater potential for development.

Summary

This chapter has focused on the whole-classroom level of analysis, and therefore began with an analysis of the classroom situation. Understanding the physical setting, social structure, and other non-obvious features of classrooms is a necessary prerequisite to understanding pupil and teacher behaviour in that context. Classrooms are busy, public places where events are multidimensional, simultaneous and unpredictable. The teacher's major role is that of organising the learning environment and managing activities: conceiving and exercising the role in this way reduces the extent to which teachers feel themselves personally to be the sole course of control.

From this perspective, various levels of the phenomenon of classroom disruption were examined. The rare event of whole-class disruption may be founded on particular interactions with one teacher, or on a class reputation with a number of teachers. Strategies for examining these were discussed. With the more common event of part-class disruption, an examination of the roles which pupils play towards each other and how they may vary across situations, can lead to creative possibilities. A particular format was offered.

Coping with classroom disruption does not always mean focusing on pupils, so the section on classroom management issues has examined the teacher's use of physical setting, social structure and learning activities. This led to an examination of how the teacher negotiates her/his view of the classroom, how confrontations can be de-escalated, how the informal rules are communicated and changed, and how a responsive climate is developed in a classroom.

Finally, the need for staff to have time for workshops which examine classroom management issues was stated, and some of the principles for making such workshops a success were mentioned.

Suggestions for discussion/investigation

1 Look at three empty classrooms in your school and make some tentative predictions on how the physical setting will affect both pupils' and teacher's behaviour. Try to find some way of checking out your predictions.

2 Find a way of observing three classes in your school, and try to ensure that these three have different ways of arranging pupils and their working relations. What effects do you note on the behaviour of pupils and teacher? Share your notes with the colleagues involved.

3 Examine the skills listed on p 70 as those required for coping with the demands of the classroom setting. Are there others you would add which are demanded by the situation (as opposed to your predictions of the behaviour which occurs in that setting)? Which are you aware of exercising? Which do you observe your colleagues exercising?

4 If there is a class in your school which seems to be disruptive as a whole and this is the case across a number of teachers, examine critically the reputation which this class has been allocated. How was the reputation constructed? On what feature of the class has the

reputation been focused? What sorts of things (on the part of pupils and on the part of teachers) serve to maintain this reputation and what sorts of things (by teachers and by pupils) could dispel the reputation? Discuss your responses to these questions with a group of colleagues, some of whom teach the class and some of whom do not.

5 Select a sub-group of pupils in one of your classes and try describing their roles by use of the framework on p 85. Ask another colleague to do the same and compare the two descriptions, examining both similarities and differences.

6 Think of a lesson you have led in the last few weeks which you regarded as successful and enjoyable, and which you feel the pupils would have seen in a similar way. Use the questions on p 89 to examine whether any aspects of your handling of activities contributed to this success. Now take one of the questions and incorporate an experiment on that theme into your planning of one lesson next week. Identify one colleague with whom you intend to share the outcomes of your experiment.

7 The comment by Fox on p 92 was made over twenty years ago. Use it as a stimulus in a team meeting to discuss *a* whether you think it still holds *b* successful practices in the three aspects of presenting methods, checking pupil reactions, taking pupil points of view into consideration.

8 Examine the suggested principles for de-escalating given on p 93 and discuss with some relevant colleagues whether they would have had a positive impact on a recent confrontation you know of. Practice one or two of the principles through enacting a situation where confrontation is possible.

9 Observe your own and others' teaching performance, with a specific focus on how you communicate the informal rules you intend to have 'in play', and especially how you communicate changes in the rules in play. Set up an experiment to test the effect of making such communications clearer.

10 Set up an informal voluntary group meeting of colleagues who wish to examine processes in classrooms and classroom management. Spend some time sharing with the group whatever came out of the investigations and discussions you have carried out. Set the themes for future agendas by eliciting the group members' priorities on a list of topics such as that on p 96. Remember that the classroom level of analysis does not give a main focus to organisational or individual features.

4   The whole individual perspective

Outline

This chapter considers the individual pupil. It starts by looking at the features of situations, and interactions in those situations, as a way of developing an understanding of individual behaviour. From this perspective it moves to the individual pupil whose behaviour causes concern and a consideration of diagnostic thinking about behaviour. It goes on to show how a group process of diagnostic thinking about behaviour, based on teachers' responses to specific diagnostic questions, can lead teachers to more elaborated understandings of pupil behaviour, resulting in strategies which are more effective. The final part of the chapter concentrates on some possible family effects on individual pupil behaviour in school and considers when it may be helpful to elicit and use information from the family context.

We are assuming that the reader will have already read the previous chapters and will therefore be aware of the effects that factors at the organisational and classroom process levels can have on the behaviour of an individual. This chapter focusing on the individual is deliberately placed here.

We believe that there is often a too hasty emphasis on the individual which can lead to other more large-scale effects being overlooked. This should be kept in mind while reading this chapter and certainly when trying out any of the suggestions for practice.

Making sense of a pupil's behaviour

The behaviour of individuals varies significantly across situations and this variation results from the interaction between the person and the particular situation (and the elements which contribute towards the uniqueness of that situation). Therefore behaviour is not the product solely of personality, dispositions or traits.

The model of the person underlying the approach adopted in this book is an interactionist model which views the complex features of the situation, with which the individual interacts, as the important factors in understanding how and why the individual opts for one form of behaviour rather than another in a particular situation. This contrasts with an individual model of the person, which locates the causes of behaviour in the internal makeup of the individual – in personality, dispositions or traits for example. This is not to say that there are no aspects of the psychological makeup of an individual which are in some form constant across situations. But the argument proposed here is that the interactionist model is a more powerful one for the teacher than the individual model because it has more relevance to the classroom situation: it offers the teacher a way of understanding pupil behaviour, and an intervention approach that fits readily into classroom organisation and routines. So, by analysing features of the situation, and how the individual interacts with those, the teacher can work out how to adapt situations so that the pupil has more choices about how s/he might behave in them.

In contrast, the approach which locates cause for behaviour *within* the person leads to descriptions of the pupil which tend to be fixed, dispositional or personality trait descriptors such as, for example, the label 'aggressive' as in 'John is aggressive'. This implies that John is an aggressive sort of person and that aggression is something inside the person. An expectation of aggressive behaviour from John is created, which can affect the way other people think about and act towards John, and in this way can be self-fulfilling of aggressive behaviour from John.

Another major drawback for the teacher in using these within-the-person explanations of an individual's behaviour is the implication they have for interventions, that is they lead logically to individual forms of intervention such as different forms of counselling or therapy. These interventions might be carried out with groups of individuals, but more usually they would be in a one-to-one setting. They would also most commonly be carried out by professionals with relevant forms of training, ie 'John needs help from a counsellor or psychotherapist.' In general these professionals would be found in agencies outside the school and therefore John would need to be referred outside the school. This, in itself, takes the initiative for working for change out of the hands of the teacher and colludes with the notion of the skilled expert who is located outside the school. This can lead teachers to feeling unskilled in these areas, and to viewing an individual pupil (such as John in this example) as a 'special', 'different' or 'disturbed' person who needs 'treatment'.

Individual forms of treatment which work 'inside' the person are frequently quite lengthy processes when compared with the time scale that the teacher is working to, so John might end up going for regular treatment over a period of many months, and it is not unusual for treatment of this type to extend over a period of a year, two or even more. Additionally, the aims of these inside-the-person forms of therapy may not coincide with the teacher's concern about a pupil. So, whereas the teacher may feel most concerned about finding a solution to particular aspects of a pupil's behaviour in certain lessons, ie John calling certain pupils names in particular lessons, which leads to arguments and sometimes to fighting, the counsellor or therapist may have more of a priority towards helping the client explore his or her feelings about particular relationships which may lie outside school, such as John's feelings of rivalry towards his brother, for example. While there are occasions when such an intervention strategy is possibly appropriate and useful, such occasions are a small minority of those where a change in classroom behaviour is the criterion of success, and this strategy does not therefore prove as useful as is often hoped by the teacher and the pastoral team. Other alternatives are therefore required which address the problem more directly, involve the teacher in developing solutions and have direct effects on classroom behaviour.

Using the interactionist model the intervention relates directly to the situation (or situations) in which change is desired, ie the lessons in which John name-calls, argues and fights, and in that sense it is highly school- and classroom-focused. It also locates the teachers, who are part of the situation in which change is desired, as possible agents of change. In this way the interactionist approach is one which is potentially teacher-friendly: teachers are valued as skilled practitioners in analysing behaviour, in developing understandings of how certain forms of behaviour can become chosen by certain pupils, and in modifying situations in order to provide pupils with increased options over their behaviour. Using this approach, John's teachers work together to reach a more detailed understanding of the situations where he acts in ways which cause disruptive effects so that they can work out strategies towards changing this.

When analysing behaviour from this perspective an exploration is made of the features of the situation which have most effect on the individual's choice of behaviour. The important features of the situation which will need to be considered will be discussed in three parts.

1 ● *Significant others* who play a part in the situation.
  ● Their *expectations* of the individual and the *reputation* they accord him or her.
  ● The *interactions* they have with the individual and how these interactions arise, and to what extent they trigger or set off responses in the individual.
2 ● The individual's *expectations* of significant others.
  ● The *view of self* that s/he seems to be presenting in a particular

situation when s/he behaves in a particular manner.
3 ● The *function* of the individual's behaviour.

The notion of the *significant other* is crucial to the interactionist perspective. It is based on the recognition that other people have an effect on an individual and on his or her behaviour, and that this effect depends on the importance accorded them by that individual, ie the extent to which s/he views them as significant. The significant other may be a peer or an adult and may be regarded positively or negatively. Thus, the key to the extent of the effect on the individual relates to the degree of regard felt by that individual for the other, irrespective of whether that is experienced as like or dislike. Teachers may or may not be significant others for particular pupils, but pupils almost always are significant to each other (whether because of like or dislike), and some are more significant than others.

The *expectations* of significant others, as we know, can have an effect on behaviour, and this too can be in a positive or a negative direction, depending on the expectation. The teacher who expects bad behaviour of an individual pupil is more likely to call out that form of behaviour in the pupil than the teacher who expects good behaviour. More than the teacher's expectations, however, the expectations of peers can be a powerful influence. If, for example, a pupil has a reputation among other pupils of being a joker and a teacher-baiter, s/he may work hard to maintain that role in order to fulfil peer expectations. This will be especially marked when the maintenance of that role links into the individual's standing among his/her peers. It may be the sole source of peer status for that individual, and in such a case it is not surprising that the pupil will work hard to sustain it.

Interactions which are initiated by significant others may start a chain of events which can be 'triggers' to an individual's behaviour. When the significant other is a fellow pupil, these initiating interactions may be deliberately aimed at setting off predictable patterns of behaviour. In these instances the individual may be 'set up' by his peers to behave in particular ways. This tends to occur when the individual's behaviour serves a function for the group. For example, the pupil who has a reputation for arguing with the teacher may be encouraged by other pupils to do so because of the entertainment value of this behaviour and/or because of its potential for diverting the teacher from the task in hand.

In some instances the triggering effect may be less deliberately aimed towards eliciting particular behaviours in the individual, and may be more of an inadvertent side effect of particular interactions with peers. Sometimes even the teacher can unwittingly provide that triggering initiative or on other occasions s/he may be aware of this potential effect but unable at the time to think of alternative styles of interaction which could avoid it as, for example, with the pupil who has a reputation among his peers for arguing with the teacher. This pupil could be precipitated into arguing if the teacher were to put an added pressure on the group, say, for more homework (which may have resulted from the teacher's recent concern about last year's poor exam results) or the pupil may react argumentatively when the teacher asks him/her publicly about some aspect of his/her work which the pupil is anxious about. Both of these teacher-initiated interactions could trigger particular forms of behaviour, in this case, arguing with the teacher.

The individual's expectations of others can also be a powerful factor in the situation. It may be that s/he expects a particular response from other pupils or the teacher, and having called out this particular response in the other s/he then reacts to it. For example, the pupil who expects to get into trouble may behave in a guilty and furtive manner which, in itself, is sufficient to arouse the suspicions of the teacher, which in turn confirms for the pupil that trouble is brewing, and so on in a spiralling pattern of escalation.

The *view of self* that the individual seems to be presenting in any situation frequently links with reputation and forms of status or standing in the group (which may not always be obvious when that status seems low). However, the need to present oneself in particular ways may reflect feelings of anxiety about *who* one shall be and *how* one shall be that sort of person. This is a particular concern for pupils of secondary age, who will be experimenting in any case with ways of presenting themselves which are consonant with the person they feel they want to be. Peer status is not as important here as the evocation of responses from others which confirm the view of self. The pupil who is concerned to appear tough may repetitively behave in a manner that is consonant with maintaining this public image. The pupil who views him/herself as a 'champion' of others will work to maintain that self picture. The pupil who rejects the identity s/he feels s/he is given by being placed in a particular group will work to maintain his/her preferred view of him/herself in spite of the disapproval of other peers. In each case the crucial factor is the view of self maintained by the individual, whether it attracts high or low status.

In order to understand behaviours we need to view them in the context of their related effects. The effect of certain chosen forms of behaviour illuminate the *function* of these behaviours. Taking the example of the pupil who behaves as if s/he is helpless, the function of this behaviour may be to activate others who then help. If 'successful' over time, a pattern of interaction may be established which augments the pupil's helpless behaviour so that it is reinforced and repeated. The function of behaviour is not always easy to ascertain, however, and the gain from behaving in a particular way may not always be obvious.

These points are illustrated in the following example. In this case, Handan is rather an isolate in the class. She would like to be part of one of the groups in the class but always seems to be on the periphery of things, with no friends. Accordingly she behaves in a way that attracts bullying from one group of pupils in the class so that this bullying will be noticed by another group of pupils who will protest about it. The gain for Handan from this sequence of events is the show of concern by the pupils who protest (the group she would like to be a part of). In actual fact, Handan is no closer to anyone as a result of all this and so she repeats the behaviour which attracts the bullying, and the whole chain repeats and could continue indefinitely. Superficially, it would seem to be a simple case of bullying which might be tackled through an approach to the group who are doing it. This approach would, however, miss out on the part Handan was playing in behaving in ways that attracted bullying. Additionally, the function of the behaviour, which was to elicit a show of concern from others as a substitute for closer peer relationships, would also be missed. It is clear that the function of an individual's behaviour is likely to be complex, and careful analysis is required in order to avoid overly simplistic explanations.

Taking the interactionist approach, which examines the range of factors within a situation, it is possible to reach an understanding of the behaviour of an individual which is complex and at the same time suggestive of possibilities for change. It is a particularly appropriate model for teachers in schools since the possibilities for change are to be found in the context of the situation in which the behaviour is being described, ie the school and the classroom.

Diagnostic thinking about behaviour

When the teacher wishes to understand better the behaviour of an individual pupil it will be useful to engage in a process of diagnostic thinking about that behaviour, based on the interactionist model as described above.

The usual context for the word diagnostic is a medical or quasi-medical one, relating to a process of identification and classification of a disease or syndrome. In the context of this book we are referring only to the thinking process, and not to an end point of classification. So, before proceeding, it will be worthwhile reflecting briefly on what diagnostic thinking is and is not.

Diagnostic thinking, in this context, is not about finding a cateogory or label to apply to forms of behaviour or individuals. It is, rather, a process of reaching a more differentiated view of pupil behaviour by exploring significant factors within the situation through a selected set of questions (cf Hamblin, 1984). The important questions which follow from the model we have outlined are the following:

- What precipitates the behaviour?
- How are others involved and what are their expectations?
- What is the individual's reputation in this setting?
- What does the individual actually do that causes concern and what view of self does s/he seem to be presenting when s/he behaves in this way?
- In what situations does s/he *not* behave like this and what view of self does s/he present then?
- What function does this behaviour serve?
- What does the individual appear to gain by behaving in this way?
- What does the individual appear to lose by behaving in this way?

It will also be important to consider:

- What skills does the individual use in the situation?
- What skills does s/he seem to lack in this situation?

All of these questions should help us towards a non-simplistic view of pupil behaviour and some clearer idea about the factors in the situation which are affecting her/his behaviour and which need to be changed in some way in order to make a difference. This approach can be used with a range of individuals and behaviours, from pupils who effectively isolate themselves by withdrawing to those who create disruptive effects. (The focus of this book is on the latter but the approach can be used to illuminate all forms of pupil behaviour.)

The questions posed in the preceding paragraph are aimed at helping teachers look more closely at the factors which affect behaviour. The usefulness of these questions seems to operate at different levels. On one level it seems they help because, by raising the main elements or factors within situations, attention is drawn to them and awareness is raised of their potential effects on behaviour. It is not uncommon for teachers to find that the simple fact of using these questions seems to help constructive thinking and on some occasions leads directly to the teacher making changes. At another level, the questions themselves reflect something of the complexity of human behaviour rather than reducing it (or, on the other hand, mystifying it) and are, therefore, more satisfying than questions from a more behavioural paradigm focusing on separated behaviours and on simple rewards and sanctions.

It may seem paradoxical that an approach which, superficially at least, makes things more complex, should result in things making more sense and fitting into place more simply. It has been found that a series of questions like the ones above helps in teasing out the intertwining strands which affect behaviour in a complex situation like a classroom. Once separated out, each one can be examined for its apparent influence on behaviour in a way that adds clarity to our understanding of behaviour. For example, one might find that the expectations of other pupils that one particular pupil plays the fool might be a powerful influence on him/her. One might find, additionally, that this expectation was more likely to be fulfilled when that pupil was sitting next to a certain other pupil, and that this usually occurred at a point in the lesson when s/he had completed the set task. This information could be elicited by just two of the diagnostic questions:

> What precipitates the behaviour?
> How are others involved and what are their expectations?

For any one pupil being considered, some questions will have more salience than others, and these will be different for different examples. This will become apparent as the questions are systematically worked through. The strategies to effect change in a particular pupil's behaviour will subsequently develop from those responses that seem to make most sense of his/her behaviour. This will not always happen immediately: it can be very difficult from the teacher perspective to work out what is the function of particular behaviours, or what the gain could be for a pupil in behaving in a particular way.

It is therefore important to find ways of increasing the power of diagnostic thinking. It can be enhanced by making it more of a group process, which involves surveying across a number of lessons with a group of teachers. This changes the focus from the individual lesson and the activities within it (as distinct situations which can be explored) to a broader focus of a range of lessons (as a set of situations to be surveyed). The power of the survey across lessons (as situations) arises from the greater power of a group of teachers to explore and problem-solve in a more complex fashion than the individual teacher alone can do (it is therefore more easily achieved in secondary schools). Additionally, the variety that is always found in a pupil's behaviour in different situations helps teachers move from stereotypical views of individuals. This contrasts with the picture of the teacher with a pupil who regularly behaves in a manner which causes disruptive effects, who sees the pupil in no other setting and concludes that s/he is a 'disruptive', locating the cause within the pupil (and probably in the home background). This teacher will expect that no change is possible unless someone deals with whatever it is 'inside' the pupil that is creating this behaviour. The secondary school teacher of, for example, a fifth-year pupil, who thinks like this, might very well feel helpless and give up expecting anything to change, especially as 'it is all too late'. Surveying across situations and with other colleagues can be a powerful antidote to this feeling of helplessness. It soon becomes apparent that a pupil's behaviour can vary a great deal across a range of lessons (cf Hargreaves, 1980). The very fact of that variability will start to provide the clues which will help to make sense of the pupil's behaviour, and when analysed alongside others' answers to diagnostic questions will aid in finding strategies that make a difference.

In primary schools, situations will be constituted of different activities within the school day, rather than different lessons. It may be harder to create a group diagnostic thinking exercise but the class teacher in this setting will tend, anyway, to have more of an overview of the variability in a pupil's behaviour derived from the range of learning activities used. Another colleague, then, can be helpful in the process of diagnostic thinking.

An example of a third-year secondary pupil will illuminate how diagnostic questions helped in understanding a pupil's behaviour and in developing strategies that made a difference. The pupil in question is Paul, a third-year boy in an inner city comprehensive school. Paul was referred to the local child guidance clinic early in the spring term by the head of year, for assessment and possible child psychotherapy and/or special education. The head of year was extremely concerned about Paul because of his behaviour, which caused a disruptive effect in school. She thought Paul was probably 'maladjusted', especially since he had previously been expelled from two schools in another authority. She described him then as 'demanding' and 'disruptive', 'clowning' and 'quite physical'. This school, incidentally, was not unused to handling a wide range of pupils, some with behaviour problems. In this case, however, the view seemed to be that Paul was 'beyond the pale'.

As part of the investigations into Paul's behaviour the head of year agreed to ask subject teachers to complete the diagnostic behaviour questionnaire (DBQ), see Figure 4.1. She agreed that as the school was still having to cope with Paul, while waiting for the outcome of his assessment, it was worth doing something . . . anything . . . that might help. The questionnaire the teachers completed (Figure 4.1) does not include all the diagnostic questions mentioned previously – deliberately so, since it was important not to overburden already busy teachers. Teachers were told, when given the diagnostic behaviour questionnaire, that the completed forms would be used as the basis of a meeting with all Paul's teachers and that the aim of the meeting would be to work together on reaching some understanding of Paul's behaviour so that strategies could be worked out and then applied in the classroom setting. It was also understood that there would probably be more than one meeting. The responses from all the completed forms were put on to a single summary sheet (Figure 4.2) so that it would be easier to look through them at the meeting.

Diagnostic Behaviour Questionnaire

To: (*Subject Teacher's name*) re: (*Pupil's name*)

From: Tutor group:

Subject: Date:

Concern has been expressed about ——'s behaviour in a number of lessons. The following diagnostic questions are designed to help us get a picture of —— across all his/her lessons so that we can make some sense of the behaviour and work out strategies to bring about change in lessons where there is concern. Whatever your view of —— I would value your answers. Thank you for your help.

What does s/he do that causes concern?

What precipitates the behaviour that causes concern?

Which other pupils are involved and what are their expectations?

What does s/he seem to gain from behaving this way?

Add any other information you feel is relevant.

Figure 4.1

In the first meeting of teachers there was a potential disaster scenario created in the opening minutes by a senior member of staff who expressed in a very forceful manner the view that the only possible solution to the problems presented by this pupil was 'to break him'. This view had some support from the form tutor who found Paul impossible to deal with. In spite of this apparently negative start the meeting proceeded as planned, ie to try to make some sense of Paul's behaviour and to work out possible strategies for change. It became clear from looking through the responses from subject teachers that there was quite a difference between some lessons and others in how Paul behaved. Even between the lessons in which there was concern it seemed that his behaviour varied (see Figure 4.2 *Forms of Behaviour*). From the list of precipitating factors and discussion it seemed that the behaviour that caused concern was set off more by aspects of teacher–pupil interaction, ie by teacher contact or lack of teacher contact with Paul, than by other factors. This seemed paradoxical but gradually it became evident that for this young man interaction with the adult present (the teacher) was more significant than with any other(s). It seemed that Paul had developed ways of initiating or extending teacher contact that were extremely successful but which in most situations created disruptive effects. Additionally, it seemed, for Paul, that apparently unrewarding interactions with the teacher were preferable to no interactions at all. There was also clearly a strong peer expectation that Paul would behave in this way, but he seemed to have no particular identifiable friends or groups of mates. By behaving in the manner described, Paul seemed able to maintain status amongst peers in general, but this seemed a secondary function. Primarily, Paul's behaviour resulted in an increase in teacher contact and so this, apparently, was its main function. Paul evidently found any form of teacher contact more rewarding than none at all and gained it by behaving in this way.

It was noted by several teachers that Paul always arrived early at his lessons. This observation led to the formulation of a strategy that proved successful in spite of, or more probably because of, its simplicity. Paul was to be acknowledged when he arrived for his lesson by addressing him personally but briefly.

Not all the teachers present felt they wanted to do this (the senior teacher and form tutor excluded themselves). A few teachers decided that in addition to this they would also try to make a point of engaging Paul in brief conversations around the school. One teacher (the science teacher) decided he would give Paul the opportunity of helping him with some of the laboratory preparation on a regular weekly basis as an additional out-of-lesson contact.

Figure 4.2 Diagnostic behaviour questionnaire summary sheet – Paul G. Third-year pupil

Lesson	Precipitators of behaviour (that causes concern)	Forms of behaviour (that causes concern)	Other pupils' involvement and expectations	Gains for the pupil from this behaviour	Additional information
1	1 Being asked to do something by the teacher. 2 Being talked to directly by the teacher.	Mostly – clever replies to adults and peers. Occasionally – physical.	Some other boys expect him (1) to play the fool, ie make them laugh (2) to stick up for himself.	Makes others laugh and gains their respect.	
2	1 Being left alone. 2 Others are watching him and expecting him to misbehave.	1 Asking pointless questions. 2 Asking for help. 3 Making a noise.	1 Others expect him to say ridiculous things and ask pointless questions. 2 Others will start being disruptive, knowing Paul will join in.	Gains admiration of certain members of the class.	
3	Teacher spending time on other pupils.	1 Swaggers round the classroom. 2 Bullies anyone smaller. 3 Swears vociferously and ostentatiously.	A minority get a kick out of the atmosphere of anarchy he creates.	Gaining an audience. Gaining a reputation for being hard. Creating an atmosphere of anarchy.	
4	Any chance for attention.	1 Loud showing off (not aggressive but very demanding). 2 Laughter. 3 Cracking jokes. 4 Prodding.	He is expected to be the clown by a small group. Peers are always involved: he 'bounces off' them.	Attention – he likes to know he is liked.	He warms very quickly if I show that I appreciate and enjoy his company. I believe he is brighter and sharper than he lets on. There is very little malice attached to his actions in class. There is also very little thought about consequences of his actions but that is by no means unique to him.

5	Arrives at the lesson already triggered.	1 Makes loud comments. 2 Passes remarks to those around him. 3 Produces back chat and comments behind T's back.	A small group in the class look to him for leadership in being disruptive.	Admiration of other peers. Amusement of other peers. Tittering of girls at his more outrageous remarks.	Always appears contrite on a one-to-one basis, although one would be a little more convinced of his serious intentions if he would avoid grinning in a rather inane way.
6	Only disruptive on one occasion. Triggered by dispute between Paul and another boy about a piece of property.	Works well and co-operates, brings out his book to ask questions far more often than most children. On one occasion refused to work, mostly silent, occasional venomous asides to other children.	Sits alone. Class takes no special notice, though aware he is potentially difficult.	Considers himself able in German and sets store by his reputation. Loves to occupy the attention of the teacher.	
7	1 Work of demanding nature requiring high-level work or long span of concentration. 2 Interaction with other pupils. 3 Inability to accept criticism. 4 Sometimes no obvious reason.	1 Raises unrelated issues in P-T and P-P interaction. 2 Will not admit his mistakes.	Other pupils involved in conversation with Paul. Some see him as a leader.	He becomes the centre of attraction. He thereby diverts attention from his work, which is often not of an acceptable standard.	
8	No disruptive incidents.	Interested, responsive, most motivated in group.			

When the next meeting of the group took place about a month later there had been a marked change in Paul's behaviour. Some felt that something must have happened at home to make such a difference! There was no evidence, however, of any change in Paul's circumstances other than the changes at school, ie the strategies that had been implemented. A term later the change was maintained and Paul was viewed as a quiet and thoughtful pupil. A year later the change continued.

This case neatly demonstrates how the variability in a pupil's behaviour across situations, ie lessons, can provide keys for teachers' generating more effective interactions (especially when other factors within the situation are also taken into account). It also demonstrates the important principle of minimum intervention in the strategy chosen. That is to say, more elaborate and time-consuming strategies were rejected in favour of one that involved as many teachers as possible in a *simple* course of action that was easily achievable.

In the example of Paul, the questionnaire that was sent round to teachers did not ask about strategies that teachers found useful. The inclusion of such a question can, however, be helpful and illuminating. Developments of the DBQ include such a question so that by the time a DBQ meeting is arranged there are already a range of strategies available for discussion. A useful series of questions to include in a DBQ is as follows:

1 What does s/he do that causes concern?
2 What precipitates this behaviour?
3 Which other pupils are involved and what are their expectations?
4 What does s/he mean to gain by behaving this way?
5 What strategies do you find are effective in either dealing with occurrences of this behaviour or encouraging other forms of behaviour?
6 What else do you think may be relevant in reaching some understanding of this pupil's behaviour?

Handling a meeting of teachers discussing an individual pupil

There are specific tasks that need attention if the meeting of teachers discussing an individual pupil who causes concern is to have the best chance of an effective outcome. These are:

• preparing for the meeting;
• providing a focus for and facilitating the meeting;

• formulating conclusions, strategies and follow-up.

The skills needed will range from communicating to individual staff over the aims of the exercise, in order to engage them as active contributors and participants, to handling a group problem-solving process where the focus is the pupil whose behaviour causes concern.

The main resource needed is the inevitable and difficult-to-find resource of time, ie when all the subject teachers involved with the pupil plus form tutor and head of year or house can be available to meet together.

The teacher organising the Diagnostic Behaviour Questionnaire meeting will also need time to distribute, collect and transcribe the DBQs completed by individual teachers on to a summary sheet for the meeting, and to ensure that other staff not able to attend the meeting are informed about any strategies being tried and of how the effectiveness of any planned strategies is to be checked out.

There will be little demand on other resources other than some facility for reproducing the DBQ summaries.

Preparing for the meeting

It is important when setting up a meeting using Diagnostic Behaviour Questionnaires to make sure that teachers are clear about the purpose of the meeting, ie to develop effective strategies that teachers can use in classrooms. The strategies will be developed from working out an understanding of a pupil whose behaviour causes concern (based on the DBQs completed by subject teachers and form tutor).

The questions the teachers will be asked to make brief notes on before the meeting are those listed above. These diagnostic questions can, in themselves, initiate a more analytical approach to exploring behaviour and therefore begin the process of diagnostic thinking.

Teachers may already be used to filling in report forms on pupils whose behaviour causes concern, but reports are often not diagnostic and teachers may be unfamiliar with following them up with a meeting aimed at exploring school-based strategies. In schools where this style of meeting has been introduced it has been found that in the initial stages it is worth the time and effort of talking individually to all the teachers who are to be involved in completing the DBQs. This helps to engage them from the outset in the purpose of the meeting and to make it clear that the views of *all* teachers are equally valuable in this attempt to create a picture of some of the features of a pupil's behaviour and its effects. The individual approach also allows time to explain to colleagues the most useful style of responding to the questions in the DBQ, ie that responses are most helpful when framed in as concrete a fashion as possible. This leads away from the labelling of behaviour as 'disruptive', 'aggressive', etc (which tells us little about what the person actually does which causes concern, or in which context s/he does it), towards a more precise account of what actually happens, where, with whom and with what effects. This is the sort of account we need to encourage teachers to write, rather than more generalised summaries which tell us little about the specific pupil actions causing concern, which give us no clues as to the features of the situation triggering, maintaining, or inadvertently rewarding the pupil, and which provide little regarding the view of self that is being presented by the pupil acting in this way.

The completed DBQs can be transcribed on to one summary sheet, so that all the contributing teachers' notes can be looked through easily and speedily. Each teacher will need to be given a photocopy of the summary sheet at the start of the meeting.

Providing a focus and facilitating the meeting

It is helpful in setting a problem-solving tone for the meeting to start by clarifying aims, ie to work together to develop some understanding of the behaviour of a particular pupil who is causing concern, so that effective strategies can be identified. This understanding can, in any case, only be partial and will rely on teachers' perceptions of what happens *interpersonally* in classrooms rather than on deducing intra-personal explanations from the pupil's behaviour.

Teachers are often more used to working together on curriculum development than on classroom processes, so it will be important to create a climate in which teachers feel neither threatened (possibly because they feel they have more problems with this particular pupil than do other colleagues), nor uninterested (possibly because they feel this pupil is not a problem for them and therefore of no particular concern to them). Often there will be one or two teachers who feel so angry and negative about the pupil that they have difficulty, initially, in joining in a diagnostic thinking exercise of this type. It is not uncommon to have a resident staffroom cynic, who will play out that role within the meeting – often starting with a cynical comment about either the pupil under discussion or the aims of the meeting. This can quickly lead other colleagues to feel helpless and hopeless about change unless it is handled carefully. The old (or sometimes young) 'campaigner' – the person who views the classroom as a battlefield – can have a similar effect. This person may also tend to state his/her position early in the meeting, along the lines of 'You have got to get them before they get you', 'There is only one way to deal with pupils like these and that's to break them' and so on. The well-prepared organiser of the DBQ meeting will have some ideas beforehand of how different people may try to dominate and distort the early stages of the meeting, and will be able to handle their views and quickly move on to elicit other views, in a way that implies that a variety of viewpoints are needed, since the aim is to illuminate the complexity of human behaviour in order to reach some useful understanding of it.

A useful way of starting the meeting is to ask teachers to read through the DBQ summary sheet for five minutes or so. Diagnostic thinking is aided by providing a series of questions which will raise some of the focal areas. The example of Paul will help in clarifying this point. The reader should look through the summary sheet of the Diagnostic Behaviour Questionnaire on Paul (Figure 4.2 on p 114) bearing in mind these questions:

1 How much variability is there in what Paul does in different situations?
2 How much variability is there in the triggers to what he does?
3 How much do other pupils' expectations and their involvement seem to play a part?
4 Does he seem popular with other pupils?
5 With whom does he engage mostly during lessons?
6 What view of himself does he seem to be presenting in different lessons?

It is important to focus in Question 1 on the variability between situations, ie to what extent does he act differently in different situations (ie lessons), rather than to what extent is he the same. This leads to a consideration of the possible influence of features of each situation on the young person which might result in the observed differences. Thus, by looking at the triggers, the influence of peer expectations, the presentation of self, etc, together with the difference in behaviour, the apparent rewards for the pupil from behaving in different ways, and the strategies which seem effective, the effect of different features of the situation on the pupil's behaviour can be assessed, and a range of possible strategies can be generated. The basic premise is, therefore, that by changing some significant feature, or features, of the situation a significant difference in pupil behaviour can result. In the example of Paul it was a very minor change in teacher behaviour, ie teachers acknowledging Paul as he arrived at his lessons, which results in more acceptable classroom behaviour.

There is an important principle in this example, which is that of minimum intervention. It can be helpful to get colleagues to brainstorm about all the possible things that *could* be changed in order to achieve the desired outcome, but the more complex the plan the more likely there are to be difficulties in its satisfactory execution. It is wasteful of teacher effort to select a complex plan where a simple one will suffice. (It is worth remembering, too, that colleagues can be very sceptical about what seem to be simple solutions and may need encouragement in that direction.) The rule of thumb is to select the strategy which requires the least effort to make a difference and achieve change.

In the DBQ meeting questions focusing on aspects of the diagnostic thinking can be a helpful stimulus for colleagues. They can also help in making the transition from the customary staffroom style of letting off steam about a pupil towards a more thoughtful and constructive level of analysis. When structuring the meeting, these questions together with the DBQ summaries form the framework for discussion (after teachers have had a few minutes to read through the summaries and to make brief notes). The development of ideas is often facilitated by asking teachers to discuss initially in small groups, in pairs and fours, and then to build up from there, leaving time for whole-group discussion for the second half of the meeting. This structure allows everyone an opportunity to share ideas with colleagues before opening up the meeting and is a useful way of getting things moving. It also circumvents those colleagues who might otherwise dominate the meeting with negative and forceful views which might be unhelpful to the stated purpose.

In summary, the questions posed are designed to stimulate thinking about the variability in the pattern of behaviour across situations (subject lessons), so that teachers can begin to hypothesise about how the variability might relate to:

1 Particular triggers such as the presence or absence of certain pupils; particular events, eg arriving late; specific tasks being set; particular forms of interaction, eg being asked to do or not to do something by the teacher, etc.
2 The involvement and apparent expectations of other pupils and how the pupil might be living up to a particular reputation, eg clown, cynic, tough-nut, etc, or responding to other pupils on this dimension.
3 The view of self that the pupil is presenting when s/he behaves in the way that causes concern, and how this compares with other views of self s/he presents in other situations when s/he behaves in a way that

does not cause concern, and what this difference might be about.

4 The apparent function of the behaviour which causes concern, in terms of what happens as a result of this behaviour, and what the apparent gain might be in terms of what s/he seems to get out of behaving in this way, such as, for example, avoidance of work, increased peer status, higher levels of interaction with the teacher . . .

It is worth noting here that sometimes it is difficult for colleagues to recognise that a pattern of teacher–pupil contact comprising negative interactions can be a powerful source of reward for some pupils. This is particularly the case for those pupils who are strongly oriented towards adults but who find few legitimate ways of establishing consistent and frequent points of contact except through behaviour which causes a disruptive effect. A recognition of this, together with a selection of other features of the situation can lead to a fairly simple yet effective strategy. With Paul it was the simple strategy of acknowledging him when he arrived for lessons. This was to be carried out in a fairly low key and consistent fashion. One or two teachers proposed, also, making a point of acknowledging Paul when they saw him around the school. These strategies, adopted by most of Paul's teachers, were apparently successful with a pupil hitherto considered maladjusted. Paul's inner-city school was not inexperienced in dealing with pupils whose behaviour produced a disruptive effect; the effects of his behaviour should not therefore be underestimated. However, the improvement in behaviour was swift and was maintained at a term's and then a year's follow-up, in spite of or possibly because of, the simplicity of the chosen strategy.

Undoubtedly the process of diagnostic thinking and related discussion in itself leads to an elaboration of teachers' views about a pupil. This in turn leads to more elaborated responses to him or her from teachers. The simple strategy thus produced is, therefore, in one sense a shorthand of a more complex grasp of a pupil's behaviour. The meeting focusing on a diagnostic behaviour questionnaire in this way provides the setting in which such understandings of a pupil's behaviour can be explored and effective strategies developed. Most teachers find the focus on interaction and classroom processes illuminating and rewarding: it allows them to take a perspective on behaviour in classrooms, to develop more understanding of the multi-dimensionality of classrooms, and to develop and share skills to help them towards greater effectiveness in their management of classrooms.

It cannot be overstressed that an important skill for the organiser of this process is to be able to give all participants the opportunity to share their views. This sharing can best be provided through the structuring of the meeting as already suggested. The organiser will need to be aware, nevertheless, that some colleagues will need more encouragement to contribute their views, while others will tend to hold forth at great length if not encouraged to be more brief. Some will quickly grasp that diagnostic thinking is clearly not about arriving at the absolute 'truth' about a person and will be constructive, flexible and creative in their thinking, while others will be more stuck with notions of maladjustment and solutions which rely on bringing in the expert. The skill of the person organising and leading the meeting will be to use those contributions which help to move the meeting forward towards a more complex understanding of the factors involved in the pupil's behaviour and thence to related strategies. At the same time s/he will have to deal in an efficient way with the teachers who epitomise the cynic, the soldier in the trenches, and the angry and hopeless – and all this without losing the positive tone of the meeting. It is often the case the the power that any of these characters potentially wield works to create a feeling of powerlessness in the group by raising anxiety. It can be helpful at these times to acknowledge the feelings that seem to be around, while at the same time helping to keep the focus of the group on the practical task in hand.

Formulating conclusions, strategies and follow-up

At the end of the meeting conclusions should be formulated. These conclusions will be based on hypotheses about the features of the situation which seem to be having an effect on the pupil's behaviour, the meaning the pupil appears to be making of the situation and the apparent function of the pupil's behaviour.

Strategies will be developed from these conclusions and will incorporate the relevant parts of those strategies which are already successful. Although it is useful during the meeting to encourage colleagues to generate as many different strategies as possible, at the conclusions stage of the meeting the minimum intervention approach should be invoked so that any strategy adopted fits readily into usual classroom routines and organisation. Strategies discarded at this stage can always be re-evaluated at a later date if required.

Solutions or strategies which involve outside experts can to some extent be explored if they arise during the meeting but it is more productive in terms of developing expertise in diagnostic thinking about classroom processes and skills in classroom management to keep the emphasis on interaction (pupil–pupil, pupil–teacher, teacher–pupil) in the classroom. This locates the power for change in the classroom teacher rather than the outside expert, and locates the problem and its resolution in the situation in which it occurs.

When the conclusions are formulated and strategies agreed on, the next step is to communicate these to staff who were not able to attend the meeting so that some consistency of approach over strategies can be adopted by all those teachers who have contact with the pupil. This is not to suggest that all colleagues should adopt the same strategy in an identical manner. Each will fit the strategy to their own way of organising and managing their own classroom. But all should be encouraged to have a sense of the importance of their contribution to the success of the work.

It will be necessary to set a time limit on the implementation of the strategies so that colleagues can meet again to evaluate the outcome and to make modifications and re-interpretations as necessary. Some fine tuning can be useful during the initial implementation period to ensure that the strategies adopted retain flexibility. But generally speaking there should be an understanding that agreed strategies will be maintained until the next meeting.

If the problem behaviour subsides, teachers may feel less inclined to attend a follow-up meeting. A common experience when there are positive changes in the effects of a pupil's behaviour is for staff to attribute this to factors beyond their control – to some change in home circumstances, for example. It is therefore well worth setting a date for the follow-up and emphasising its importance so that, when there are positive outcomes as a result of the diagnostic thinking exercise, the teachers involved can be encouraged to reflect on their effectivness in that group problem-solving exercise. This will pave the way for future meetings in the same style.

Successful outcomes may not, however, be immediately forthcoming and this should be made clear in the initial meeting. Arranging a follow-up meeting explicitly to modify strategies on the basis of feedback can be a useful antidote to any unrealistic expectations about instant solutions. In spite of this caveat, the experiences reported from teachers engaged in these diagnostic thinking exercises are positive. It seems that the process of discussion in this style can have fairly immediate benefits for staff who engage in it. These benefits relate to overcoming the isolation and frustration that teachers experience in the face of a pupil whose behaviour causes a disruptive effect, and to an approach which encourages them to take a perspective on the features of the situation which contribute towards an understanding of pupil behaviour. This helps them to move into a proactive rather than a reactive mode in a setting in which they have peer support, and subsequently to transfer this into the classroom setting. It also has positive spin-offs in terms of the skills and understandings which are developed and are then available for use in other cases.

The running of DBQ meetings falls readily into the role of the head of year or head of house, blending the training function of the role with the exercise of the skills of handling groups of teachers. It also moves the head of year/house out of crisis intervention and into a mode which provides for colleagues the sharing and development of expertise in managing classrooms.

When and how knowledge of family is important

Readers will have noticed that there has been no mention of families so far in this chapter. This omission does not imply that the authors think that families have no influence on behaviour. Rather, it is a deliberate move to redress a tendency often found in schools to locate the cause for a pupil's difficult behaviour in home background. When this occurs there if often an accompanying view that the situation is hopeless, ie the school is powerless.

Our view is that families do indeed have a powerful influence on the behaviour of individual family members (in this case, children), but the power of situations upon the behaviour of individuals is also significant and tends to be underestimated. Teachers are in the business of managing classrooms and learning activities for their pupils, ie they are managers of situations. They are consequently in a unique position to make a study of individual pupil behaviour in different situations (as described in this chapter) and to make the kinds of changes to features of those situations which will have effects on pupil behaviour. We feel that this form of classroom-based analysis and intervention has not been developed or exercised as much in schools as it deserves (given its effectiveness).

At this point in this chapter on the whole-individual perspective, having already explored diagnostic thinking about the individual in the classroom setting, it is appropriate now to turn to the individual in the family setting and the issue of knowledge of the family, and when this may be important.

The family is undoubtedly a significant and powerful influence on the school-age child, and parental perspectives concerning school have an effect on a pupil's view of learning and on his/her engagement in the learning process. We are assuming, therefore, that the school will work in partnership with parents so as to maximise pupils' potential for success in school. The style of this partnership will vary according to the age and stage of the child. At the nursery stage one might expect regular and frequent contact through the presence of a parent or parents in the daily life of the school. At the later stage of secondary schooling, generally speaking, a different style of contact would be more appropriate (Johnson and Ransom, 1983). This would reflect the young person's developing autonomy, independence and need to establish and develop a sense of him/herself in relation to others outside the immediate family context.

The school will, therefore, be in regular contact with the home in some appropriate manner. The regularity and style of communication needs careful consideration so that, when a parent or parents are invited to come to school to help with the school's difficulty with a young person, there are already good home-school relations. On the occasions when there are school concerns it is often difficult for the parent or parents of a child who is presenting problems for the school not to feel anxious and blamed by the school for these problems. Parents are likely to feel personally ashamed and responsible for their child's behaviour and to feel defensive and/or angry as a result, or they may find it difficult to see the school's problem because there is none at home and resent the school for involving them in what, to them, seems to be the school's failure. If the school has already built up a positive and personal relationship with the family, the invitation to discuss behaviour which concerns the school will tend to be viewed more positively by the family. This will enhance the chances of effective communication between school and family. A good working partnership can then be developed in order to bring about change.

This brings us to the question of when and how knowledge of family is important. *When* can be assessed from the results of DBQs, if one or more of the following are found to apply:

1 Patterns of behaviour across situations show little variability, ie are very similar.
2 There is no discernible pay-off for the behaviour in the immediate situation.
3 It is already known that parental involvement has been important in the past for similar sorts of difficulties in school.

These will now be explored, with case examples demonstrating *how* family knowledge was important and how it was used to bring about change in pupil behaviour.

1   *Patterns in behaviour show little variability*

The general finding is that disruptive pupils are not disruptive in all situations, ie lessons, and that the behaviour with which a pupil disrupts is different in different lessons. In exceptional cases, however, a scrutiny of completed diagnostic behaviour questionnaires will show a trend towards consistency in behaviour across a range of lessons, which suggests that the differences between those situations (ie the features of different lessons) are not acting as powerfully as they generally do. This suggests some form of process which is over-riding the effect of the differences within and between situations. A common phenomenon in such cases is for the teacher to feel that the pupil concerned is already in a particular mood when s/he arrives at the lesson and/or that the pupil is seeking an opportunity to initiate or join in a chain of behaviour which predictably leads to a disruptive incident. When this occurs in a similar fashion across a range of lessons it is a possible indicator of factors outside the immediate situations which are exerting an effect on the pupil's behaviour. Before assuming a family link, however, there needs to be exploration of possible precipitating factors outside the context of lessons but still within the school situation, as, for example, in the case of a pupil who is being systematically abused or teased by other pupils between lessons. When those possibilities have been explored and eliminated as possible precipitating factors, the family dimension can be usefully explored.

An illustrative example of when family knowledge was useful and how it was used is that of Sam. When Sam started at secondary school, the view that teachers quickly developed was of a rather immature pupil, who was not very popular with other children, preferring, apparently, the company of staff. At this stage no particular problem in lessons was remarked on. Gradually, however, over the first term a pattern of behaviour emerged which created disruptive effects in the majority of Sam's lessons. One teacher's observations from the diagnostic behaviour questionnaire give a flavour of Sam's behaviour in lessons:

● crying
● refusing to work
● falsely accusing others of kicking, punching, throwing things
● hyperventilating until she goes into a panic
● making strange noises when boys walk past her while she backs into the wall.

The consistency of the pattern and the persistence with which Sam presented herself in such an odd and victimised role led to a consideration of factors outside the immediate situations. In this case, previous school records and a meeting with parents were invaluable in working out what would contribute towards effective strategies in Sam's case. Sam, it transpired, was the elder of two girls of parents who had had severe doubts about their ability to parent when Sam was a baby. From an early age Sam was viewed by her parents as a problem baby and they thought then that she would probably be difficult to rear. At that time she was, apparently, difficult to feed and to comfort. By the time she was eligible to attend nursery school her parents had such difficulty in handling Sam that they were pleased to take advantage of local pre-school provision for children who were viewed as having emotional and behavioural difficulties. For a number of years Sam was viewed as a child who needed part-time special educational provision. She was not, however, considered by the local child guidance team as being suitable for individual psychotherapy. Her parents were the focus of their input, to help them feel more competent in their parenting of Sam.

By the time Sam was of junior school age she was attending her local mainstream primary school full time. Her parents were still anxious about how she would progress, so the headteacher of the school arranged regular meetings with them approximately every half term and reported to them on positive aspects of her work, behaviour and general progress. It seems likely that these meetings gave the parents a feeling of reassurance over Sam's 'normality' and hence *their* ability to cope with her. Certainly, at this time her behaviour at school was viewed as unproblematic though 'fussy'.

When Sam moved on to secondary school the important information about regular and positive contacts with the parents was overlooked. After half a term teachers noticed odd behaviours developing. By using diagnostic behaviour questionnaires and a DBQ meeting teachers were able to establish that Sam would escalate her 'odd' behaviour if they showed her sympathy and friendliness. Effective strategies were:

- firmness not sympathy
- ignoring her
- encouraging her to conform to the standards of behaviour of the group and discouraging behaviour that was different from the group.

These classroom-based strategies coupled with a resumption of the regular contact with the parents, providing them with positive reports on work, behaviour, etc, and, through this, reassurance and implicit support led to a reduction in Sam's extreme behaviours. One set of strategies without the other would not have had the same long-term effects: the combination of the two was invaluable.

This example could be viewed in some ways as extreme, in that Sam's behaviour was quite bizarre. It was chosen deliberately in order to show the possible effectiveness of the interactionist approach, which addresses the function of behaviours rather than intra-psychic causes. Thus, the starting point for the school is the classroom and an analysis of classroom situations, ie lessons. When necessary, this approach moves out to take in factors from the wider system, ie the family. In this case, effective strategies evolved from an understanding of the relationship between the pupil, the family and the school. Sam's case also illustrates the potential trap for teachers who make judgments about an individual's degree of maladjustment or disturbance directly from the behaviour presented. If these inferences has been pursued by Sam's secondary school teachers, it is possible that they would have mounted a case to label her as maladjusted and in need of treatment and/or special schooling. Sam, however, continued in a mainstream school for the remainder of her school career and proceeded from there to a youth training scheme.

A principle in working with this approach is to hold on to the basic question: What is the function of the behaviour? ie What seems to be achieved by the person who is behaving in this way? rather than: How disturbed is the person who behaves like this? For Sam the function of her behaviour in school seemed linked to gaining concern and contact with adults, which replicated a pattern of interactions in the family. The strategy that was formulated towards the family was simple and effective and helped the parents to view Sam more 'normally' and to treat her accordingly, with benefits all round.

2   When there is no discernible pay-off for the behaviour in the immediate situation

The second major group of occasions when knowledge of the family may be important is illustrated by the example of Chris. Chris was nearing the end of his fourth year in a mixed comprehensive school when he became a problem. There was no previous history of disruptive incidents until this time, and no particular difficulties with work. In fact Chris seemed more of an irritation than a disruption. His teachers put it this way:

'He does not disrupt but disturbs by not working.'

'Shows no interest, lethargic.'

'Disruptive is not applicable. He's more like a hibernating bear.'

'Not disruptive, but reluctant to take instructions and slow working.'

The picture across the board was of a pupil who was avoiding engagement in learning in a manner that was striking in its consistency. The involvement of other pupils in all of this was minimal:

'Other pupils not greatly involved but drawn into conversations. They appear to accept his truculence and lack of motivation without imitating it.'

All the teachers were of the opinion that Chris seemed to gain little from behaving in this way and that no strategy seemed to make any difference. It was also noted that Chris was 'pleasant outside class, speaks first'.

It seemed that Chris reserved this withdrawal of co-operation and communication exclusively for lesson times and for *all* his subject teachers in those situations.

Talking with Chris individually eventually led to some clarification. Chris saw no point in being in school: he wanted to leave as soon as possible. Meeting with the parents and Chris made the picture even clearer: Chris was going to be sixteen years old at the end of the autumn term (in his fifth year), ie next term. Both Chris and his parents were under the impression that he could leave on his sixteenth birthday. They were quite convinced that they knew other young people who had done this, and who had attended this school. There was a job lined up for Chris in the family business and any delay over his starting work was an inconvenience. Teachers who had already been aware of Chris' misunderstanding had in the past tried to explain the situation to him but Chris had not trusted these explanations and had withdrawn from school lessons through passive non-co-operation and psychological truancy. He was supported in this by his parents who, by this time, were angry about negative school reports. They had never had any complaints about Chris before and they felt, therefore, that the school must be at fault. By talking through all of this and explaining the possibilities for Chris to make the best use of his remaining time in school, it was possible finally for both pupil and parents to accept the situation regarding the leaving date. In addition, adjustments were made to Chris' timetable so that some of *his* priorities for success without exams could be achieved in the time remaining. This led to an improvement in his behaviour in lessons.

Chris' case illustrates the important point that diagnostic thinking about behaviour is not an approach which reduces the teacher's workload in a simple sense. If it is applied carefully, it should indeed reduce the time subject teachers spend in class dealing with pupils who create disruptive effects. But there may be other areas of work which temporarily increase. In Chris' case there were pupil and family perceptions of school and schooling which had to be explored and worked with, and compromises made in school so that progress was possible. It was also necessary for the school to spend some time looking at what could be offered that was of relevance to this particular pupil in his final year of schooling. This meant timetable changes and arrangements for work experience, all taking teacher time and effort. It also raised questions for the school about the range and style of courses that were on offer, and to what extent the courses were constructed, taught and certified so as to maximise engagement in them for the whole range of pupils in the school. This points to another outcome of diagnostic thinking about behaviour at this level of application, to help schools to monitor a sample of individual pupils' experiences of learning (as well as working on finding individual solutions and strategies to the problems caused by pupils whose behaviour creates disruptive effects).

3   When it is already known that parental involvement has been important in the past for similar sorts of difficulties in school

This condition (when knowledge of the family is important) may seem too obvious to be worth mentioning, on the grounds that schools will always strive to involve parents in such difficulties and that parental involvement is a good thing in principle anyway. It is, however, considered worth giving this condition some emphasis to support the position of involving parents at the *early* stage of an escalating pattern of behaviour which causes disruptive effects and of keeping them involved positively over time.

Frequently, parents are brought in only when the school feels that the pupil is beyond its control. This places the parents in the virtually impossible position of having to exercise control over the child without actually being present when authority and control breaks down. The impossibility of this task can lead parents to avoid the school altogether, to blame the school, to become excessively punitive towards the child, or to feel helpless and give up. None of these outcomes is likely to benefit the child or the school. (The two latter outcomes would also be likely to have negative effects within the family.) Early parental involvement can therefore constitute an effective strategy in itself. In recurring patterns of difficult behaviour it continues to be important.

The school career of Jo illustrates the need for parental involvement, and provides a cautionary tale, which shows what can happen when parents are not kept involved. Jo had a history of behavioural difficulties at primary school. It was noted in her primary school record that she had confrontations with teachers and other children from the time she was in the Infants. From time to time it seemed there was an improvement but then the situation would deteriorate and the recurring report appeared of Jo 'throwing something in class', 'being rude to a teacher' or 'shoving another child'. Different forms of special provision had been made at different times. Each time the situation appeared to improve and then to deteriorate. The records showed contact with Jo's mother at the Infant stage but little after that. It had been noted that Jo's mother was raising two daughters single-handed, that she was an effective parent, and that they were three lively and strong-minded characters who formed a very close family unit.

At the secondary transition stage considerable concern about Jo was communicated from the primary to the secondary school. The secondary school, it seemed, was primed to receive a difficult pupil. Jo quickly lived up to the expectations and fears of her new teachers. Her mother was asked to visit school shortly before Jo's first period of suspension because of her difficult behaviour in and out of class towards teachers and pupils. Shortly after this she was expelled from the school. In Jo's new school the headteacher, head of year and form tutor met with Jo and her mother to establish what the school viewed as acceptable behaviour from Jo. An agreement was reached which involved her mother in regular school meetings which were initially at weekly intervals. Jo's mother was extremely bitter and angry in the early stages of the discussion of this plan. Her anger was primarily directed at those teachers from the previous school who had 'kept her informed' of all the difficulties and problems Jo had caused in school over time, but who had failed to ask her to help in solving those difficulties. From her perspective it felt as though the school were blaming her for having a naughty child and therefore not being a good enough parent. For a year Jo's mother was involved with this school in planning joint strategies, monitoring their effects and reviewing their progress. After a period of intensive contact there was a reduction in the number of meetings to once a month, with some additional informal contact between form tutor and parent. At the end of that school year Jo had to move on to a Senior High School, after a consistently positive period of schooling.

In the next school regular meetings with Jo's mother were not set up. The school felt it would be preferable to 'see how Jo would settle'. The old pattern of behaviour recommenced after a few weeks and progressively deteriorated, culminating in Jo's expulsion. It seems highly likely that a more positive outcome might have resulted if the strategy of regular involvement with the mother had been continued.

This case raises a number of questions and issues – for example, how does the pastoral team strike a balance between giving pupils a fresh start and using information from the previous school? We propose that the pastoral team which is working professionally and pro-actively will be able to examine previous school records for patterns of behaviour and effective strategies, while recognising and resisting the negative effects of labelling and of negative expectations.

All of these examples illustrate the need to consult with parents over behaviour problems in school. They also show how the way parents are involved in helping needs to vary to suit the circumstances of the case. The parent's perspective on the problem may be crucial to an understanding of the pupil's behaviour and to its resolution, as in the example of Chris and his parents who believed he could leave school as soon as he was sixteen. On the other hand, it may be the parents' regular involvement with school in planning and carrying out strategies that is effective, as in Jo's case. Or the contact may be a way of modifying the parents' view of the child, as in Sam's case, in which parental involvement provided reassurance to anxious parents, whose anxiety was inadvertently contributing toward the child's view of herself as a problem and resulting in disruptive behaviour.

Thus, in a variety of ways parents can be engaged as partners in understanding and finding solutions to difficult and disruptive behaviour. Their unique and special knowledge and understanding of the child can be brought to bear in solving these school-based problems.

Summary

This chapter has tried to show how it is possible to take an individual perspective without falling into the trap of labelling a pupil and thereby helping to create and confirm a deviant reputation. The interactionist approach, which has been described here, allows the school to explore pupil behaviour and its effects through the situations in which it occurs, and to develop effective strategies from this diagnostic thinking process. Reactive forms of crisis management (frequently carried out by one individual in the management team, such as the head of year/house whose role has been distorted into one that is purely disciplinary) can thus be replaced by a problem-solving response of diagnostic thinking. Teacher teams then work together under the guidance of pastoral specialists to reach elaborated understandings about pupil behaviour and from these to formulate classroom-based strategies which can be applied, monitored, amended and evaluated in a consistent fashion.

There has also been a consideration of when and how the family perspective is of particular relevance in this process, and how family support can be invaluable in complementing the work of the school in puzzling and difficult cases. This chapter links back to Chapter 2 on the whole-school perspective and Chapter 3 on the whole-class perspective, since no analysis of pupil behaviour in school can be complete without reference to the contexts of the organisation of the school and the classroom, and the effects of these on the individual. The reader who has read this chapter first may find it most useful now to read Chapter 3 before Chapter 2. The reader who is working through the book in chapter order will find a move in the next chapter to a different focus of analysis and input, ie to the pastoral curriculum and pastoral management, and the ways that preventative strategies can be planned into the learning experiences and the management – in their widest senses – of the school.

Suggestions for discussion/investigation

1 The aim of this discussion topic is for the pastoral team to explore the effect of particular forms of language, eg labelling, on our thinking about pupils.

Take the case study of Paul on p 111, duplicate it for colleagues and discuss it; in your discussion explore:

i To what extent the language that is sometimes used to describe pupils and their behaviour, ie labels and categories, can affect the sorts of solutions we think of and what other forms of description would avoid this.

ii The extent to which the descriptions of Paul might have an effect on how an individual teacher, who had not yet met him, might view him and act towards him.

iii In what ways the pastoral team can work to reduce the amount of negative labelling and its effects.

2 The aim of this discussion topic is to develop the skills of diagnostic thinking about difficult or disruptive behaviour within the pastoral team.

Select a pupil whose behaviour causes concern in your school (not the most extreme example at this stage) and involve colleagues in completing diagnostic behaviour questionnaires using the questions from p 116.

Duplicate the following questions. Work through them with colleagues, using a *summary sheet* of all the completed DBQs.

STAGE I
- Examine:
    i the variability in the pupil's behaviour in different lessons
   ii the range of events which precipitate the difficult behaviour and the relationship between these events and the difficult behaviour
  iii the involvement and expectations of other pupils and the relation-ship between these and the difficult behaviour
   iv the view of self that s/he seems to be presenting when s/he behaves in this way
    v the range of strategies that already seem useful
   vi the possible function of the behaviour, ie what s/he seems to gain/avoid/create/initate as a result.
    (Stated in language that avoids relabelling.)

STAGE II
- As a result of the understandings reached in Stage I generate three possible strategies to change the difficult behaviour, focusing on *ii–v* above.
- From those strategies select a few that seem to satisfy the function of the behaviour, ie how can the pupil achieve the same thing without creating disruptive effects. NB If the main function of the behaviour appears to be work avoidance because of under-achievement, consider the possible need for learning support, effective study skills, etc.

    Select one strategy that requires the minimum intervention and which can be applied consistently.

STAGE III
- Evaluate the intervention after an agreed period (approximately 3 to 4 weeks) and amend on the basis of any new information that arises as a result.

3 The aim of this discussion topic is to help the pastoral team develop a variety of ways of working with parents over pupils who cause concern because of the disruptive effects of their behaviour.

    From the section *When and how knowledge of family is important* discuss the similarities and differences in handling parental involve-ment in the three case examples.

Select three pupils in your school and discuss possible similarities and differences in the styles of work that would be most effective with their respective parents.

5   The long-term contribution of the pastoral system

Outline

This final chapter examines some of the more long-term aspects of a school's pastoral functioning with regard to discipline. In particular it looks at pastoral curriculum and pastoral management.

Under pastoral curriculum the possibilities for taking a preventative approach to school discipline are discussed, after an introductory clarification of what is meant by pastoral curriculum, its learning offer (social-personal skills and knowledge for success) and the various locations for such learning (subject lessons, tutorial programmes, specialist lessons and so on). In particular, activities which could be included in a tutorial programme are given.

Under pastoral management issues are raised regarding the pastoral system and how it operates. In particular the role of the form tutor, the functioning of tutor teams and the communication of the pastoral systems are examined. In conclusion the long-term issues of staff development and evaluation are briefly discussed.

Taking a longer-term perspective

To the present point, this book has adopted a medium-term perspective on the relation between pastoral care and school discipline. In other words, it has examined the situation which exists in many schools, where considerations of discipline are placed at the door of the pastoral team. And the general approach of Chapters 2, 3 and 4 has been to examine the patterns of indiscipline which are so presented, in order to raise discussion about the range of various factors involved, not exclusively the pupil.

In adopting this perspective we have intended to address the situation where disruptive issues are brought to the door of the pastoral team, but in the long term we believe such a situation is wasteful of pastoral staff expertise, and is based on questionable underlying processes.

Therefore, in this chapter we raise issues which will remain important in the long-term relation between pastoral care and discipline and yet have not been addressed in detail in previous chapters. In so doing we intend to move away from the situation where a distorted responsibility for disruptive issues is loaded on the pastoral team, to raise the more fundamental question – what is the proper role of the pastoral system with regard to school discipline (remembering our view, stated in Chapter 1, that the phenomenon of school indiscipline will never be completely eradicated)?

Our consideration of the long-term picture is divided into two related parts: pastoral curriculum and pastoral management. The first recognises that in the school's overall personal-social learning offer to pupils, some time can be given to themes of rules and responsibilities in an organisation. The second raises similar themes in a different way for staff, and addresses roles, responsibilities and communication.

In moving from the medium-term to the long-term view, we can be explicit about our omission of the short-term. First, we regard a school's short-term responses to indiscipline as unlikely to be strongly affected by what may be advocated in books: more immediately powerful processes are often at work. Second, as was argued in Chapter 3 on classrooms, the short-term question 'What do I do about X?' can divert attention from the very factors which have had a hand in the problematic X occurring. Therefore, in omitting a detailed consideration of the short-term, we are clearly claiming that the positive contribution of pastoral care is rarely achieved through short-term demand-led responding, but through long-term consideration of the personal-social processes in a school's functioning.

Pastoral input through the pastoral curriculum

Individual cases of disruptive behaviour will inevitably require responses on the part of teachers. The responses described in Chapter 4 – *The whole-individual perspective* – are diagnostic, creative and more proactive and effective than the reactive crisis-management approaches which are so often used with individuals creating disruptive effects. They are, none the less, responses to individuals and, as such, are of their nature demand-led. Similarly, Chapters 2 and 3 on the whole-school and the whole-class perspectives describe strategies of the pastoral team which are responsive to patterns of disruption rather than pro-active. Pastoral input through the pastoral curriculum moves the work into this preventative arena.

By curriculum we mean the learning experiences on offer to pupils. We support the view that the school's curriculum, in this broad sense, will be coherent and effective in achieving its aims only if is it developed out of whole-school curriculum policies. This contrasts with piecemeal approaches to curriculum planning typified by strictly bounded subject areas, producing self-contained syllabi, which have no connection with other facets of the pupils' learning experiences. Whole-school curriculum policies would, therefore, be developed from an identification of the school's goals and would involve the detailing of aspects of the curriculum prior to schemes of work at the departmental level. They would also be subject to consultation with all the school's role partners, consumers and clients: staff, governors, parents and pupils, to ensure they had relevance and could be viewed as worth supporting.

In contrast with this broad view the potential trap for the team involved in pastoral care is inadvertently to marginalise pastoral care through the creation of pastoral programmes which are carried out solely in tutor time, which can be viewed as time-fillers of little relevance, and which masquerade as a pastoral curriculum.

Given that the broad aim of pastoral care is to help pupils benefit more extensively from their school experience, the pastoral curriculum is one particular and broad aspect of pastoral care. It is that aspect which focuses on the pupil and their learnings about themselves as pupils within the organisation of the school, as learners, as members of a wider community, and as future citizens. This broad description has been conceptualised by Watkins (1985) in a thematic fashion which emphasises developing aspects of the self as:

- the bodily self
- the sexual self
- the social self
- the vocational self
- the moral/political self
- the self as a learner
- the organisational self

  (Developed from Wall, 1974, and Hamblin, 1978, 1981)

These themes could be used to organise the content of the learnings on offer through the pastoral curriculum in order to promote pupils' personal and social development and their success as learners in school. The achievement of this aim would, we believe, have a powerful effect on pupil behaviour in school. Undoubtedly, some pupils would still come to feel disaffected toward school, but this would probably be a less significant number than is currently the case (and many of these, we feel, would probably respond to curriculum reforms to increase relevance and motivation in secondary schools).

Curriculum planning requires a careful analysis of where and how the learning experiences are to be offered. There is a range of possible locations available:

- tutorial programmes
- specialist guidance lessons
- subject lessons

- extra-timetable activities
- residential experience
- work experience
- para-curriculum of classroom and school
- community links.

Each location will tend to have particular features which are intrinsic to that location and which make it more suitable than another for a particular aspect of a theme within the pastoral curriculum. Other considerations will be to do with which teaching teams are most appropriate, which teaching styles best suited to aspects of themes, and when personal knowledge of the pupil both as an individual and as a member of the class group over time is especially useful. With the spiral curriculum notion in mind, the timing of the introduction of a particular topic and the way it is revisited over time can also be worked on. These are all inter-related issues which will need to be explored so that decisions can be made in a planned and co-ordinated way. This will undoubtedly need cross-curricular team work.

For instance, an outcome of such planning could be that the theme of sexual self was addressed through:

- specific subject lessons, such as biology, and learnings about the physical structures and functions of the reproductive system.
- other subject lessons, such as English literature, art and drama, history, geography, politics, sociology, psychology, economics, etc, and learnings about views of sexuality, gender identity, sex roles and behaviour, within particular historical, geographical, political, social contexts.
- specialist guidance lessons, such as health education, and learnings about those aspects of sexual behaviour and sexuality concerned with sex roles and stereotyping, and with related aspects of physical and psychological health.
- tutorial programmes, and learnings about the relationship aspects of sexual behaviour, gender identity, and ways of counteracting roles based on stereotyping.
- para-curriculum of classroom and school, and positive or negative learnings about the flexibility of roles through how boys and girls are treated equally, or differently, by teachers in class and around the school; through equality in the amount and style of talk directed to boys and girls in class; through the absence of sex stereotypes in the published materials used, or else the critical appraisal of this sort of material if it is in current use; through the teacher's attitude to

incidents of sexual harassment between opposite sex pupils and between teachers; through the teachers demonstrating equality in expectation of achievement generally towards the sexes; through positively encouraging achievement in traditionally sex-linked subjects for members of the other sex, and so on.

All of these learning experiences in the different locations in this particular example would be inter-related so that no single aspect became unintentionally isolated and inadvertently over-emphasised or over-simplified.

The reader may at this point be wondering about the relevance of this particular example to the main theme of school discipline. In a general sense it is demonstrable that the conceptualisation of the pastoral curriculum into inter-relating aspects of self implies a connection between personal-social development and success and achievement in school, and in that sense the relevance is clear. Additionally, we suggest that the sexual aspect of the self (and the related physical or bodily self) is one which tends to be of greater concern to pupils at the secondary stage of their school career than it has been previously, and certainly it has been shown that sex role stereotypes can have powerful effects on pupils' views of themselves as learners, on their relationships, their self-presentation, their achievement, and on teachers' treatment of them in classrooms. These understandings and approaches are, therefore, important and may help to work against some of the powerful gender-related patterns of disruption (discussed in Chapter 1).

Having looked at the potential breadth of the pastoral curriculum in terms of its possible content and locations, we will turn now to consider the location which has specific relevance for the pastoral team in general and the form tutor in particular, the tutorial programme. The assumption is made that the tutorial programme will form one location for delivering the pastoral curriculum. It has particular advantages for certain aspects of themes where the tutor's knowledge and relationship with the pupil may be more important. For example, when the aim is to promote self-knowledge and inter-personal skills it can be helpful for the pupil to explore social and familial processes in a cumulative and continuous fashion and in a learning environment which has developed over time as a safe scenario for self-reflections and personal exploration. The form tutor is in the key position as far as facilitating this environment and this area of learning goes. Other subject specialists may encourage a similar process, using fictional or real stories and histories, analogies, parallels, personal experiences, relevant examples and illustrations. Even so, those subject-based opportunities do not always offer quite the same possibilities for self-reflection and personal growth as the tutor period can.

As to methods, activity-based learning is certainly not, and never was, the prerogative of tutors and the tutorial programme. Nevertheless, it seems clear that these methods have particular application and relevance to the content of the tutorial programme (Watkins, 1981), whereas in other areas of the curriculum there may be a different range of teaching style and presentation in order to match the subject content and learning process.

In our model school the activities of the tutorial programme would be decided on as part of a whole-school approach to curriculum planning, in which the pastoral curriculum was an integral part. For the purposes of this book, however, we are prepared to assume that the outcome of such planning in many schools would include some attention being given in tutor periods to the theme of discipline. Therefore, examples of possible activities for the tutorial programme will be presented. It is assumed that the reader who wishes to try out any of these activities in the home-school setting will subject them to critical appraisal, involving other colleagues in the pastoral team in this process, so that they can be amended to suit the context in which they will be used. We feel sceptical about the value of activities which are used without being subjected to this process and therefore urge teacher colleagues to resist any inclination in that direction.

Thre is a range of possible content areas for activities in the tutorial programme which would contribute towards school discipline. These can be grouped under the headings of 'self as a learner' and 'organisational self' and could be elaborated further from the sample list provided and worked into inter-relating activities designed to help pupils explore, for example:

- self as a learner
- attitudes to learning
- skills for effective study
- relationships with peers in learning situations
- teacher styles and expectations
- parental expectations with regard to learning and schooling
- self in relation to the school as an organisation
- rules in school.

A significant feature of school life little emphasised in a pro-active sense in tutorial programmes is that of rules in school. Indiscipline in school frequently constitutes a breach of formal or informal rules. The centrality of rules in pupil's accounts of disruptive incidents supports this (Tattum, 1985). Consequently, it is worth considering carefully how the school rules at both the formal level (in terms of those written down), and the informal level (in terms of the unwritten rules of the classroom), can be examined by pupils in the tutorial programme.

Interpreting school to pupil – activities which focus on rules

Most schools have a set of rules which are written down. Some are phrased in general terms, whereas others are highly specific about particular behaviours. However these rules are framed they can be regarded seriously by the school staff and breaches of these rules are often viewed as constituting incidents of indiscipline.

These written rules we have referred to as the formal rules, in contrast to the informal (not written down) rules. There are informal rules which each teacher develops for him or herself in order to manage the pupils' learning environment in the way s/he as an individual finds most effective in the context of that particular school. In most schools there is some level of agreement among teachers about how the formal rules are to be interpreted and applied (although the level of agreement over this will undoubtedly vary across schools). Class teachers' informal rules, on the other hand, can appear to vary enormously from one person to another, and this variation can be found within the same department, let alone the same school. These informal rules are seldom, if ever, written down, yet incidents of indiscipline in classrooms are frequently breaches of the teacher's informal rule system. Both forms of rules deserve attention in the tutorial programme.

First, we will consider the formal rules. In most situations where sets of written rules exist they tend to be framed with a particular view of the welfare of the community and the aims of the organisation. Rules are, however, a form of imposition, and the degree to which they are kept voluntarily by the members of a community will depend on the extent to which they feel inclined to co-operate with them, and the extent to which they can be meaningfully enforced. Many teachers prefer not to work in schools in which their predominant role is one of policing and enforcing school rules. This leads us back to engaging the inclination to co-operate, and to a consideration of how the pupil's inclination to co-operate can be actively encouraged and developed.

Most people would agree that when they can see the point of a rule or regulation, and when they feel it makes sense in the context in which it is applied, they will tend to co-operate with it. Furthermore, when they have been involved in making that rule, they will actively support it. In order to understand, co-operate with, and actively support school rules pupils will need opportunities in the tutorial programme for examining the rationale for rules in a general sense and the specific rules the school has in operation. The school as an organisation will need to have obvious mechanisms which demonstrate to pupils that consideration can be given to proposals for amendments to rules. These themes are clearly not for presentation as once-and-for-all activities (indeed, we doubt that any themes in the pastoral curriculum can be usefully treated in that way) but can be revisited at appropriate stages in the pupils' school career. Some examples of possible activities related to the school rules theme follow.

1　Activity – Rules in organisations

Timing This activity would take place over three linked tutor periods as part of a series on *Rules in School*.

Aim The aim of this activity is to help pupils examine rules in a variety of organisations as a step towards helping them examine the formal rules in their own school.

SESSION 1

Tasks – The tutor explains the aim of the activity to the pupils.
 – The pupils are asked to carry out a survey into rules in a variety of organisations.
 – Each pupil is asked to interview a relative or friend, asking them a series of set questions (see *Survey* below) and making note of their answers. The tutor goes over the questions to make sure every pupil understands them.
 – Each pupil is asked to bring their notes back to a particular tutor period to share their findings with other pupils.

Rules in organisations – survey

　　i Name an organisation, eg firm, business, club, etc that you are or have been a member of.
　　ii How big is the organisation and what is its purpose?
　　iii Are there any rules or regulations that you have to abide by as a member of the organisation?
　　iv What are those rules or regulations about?
　　v How do you know what the rules are?
　　vi What happens if someone breaks a rule?
　　vii Do all members of the organisation abide by these rules?

SESSION 2

Tasks– Pupils are organised into pairs to share their findings.
- They are asked to look for similarities and differences in their pairs in:

  - the type of organisation (its size and purpose)
  - the rules themselves
  - what the rules are about
  - how the rules are communicated
  - the outcome of rule-breaking.

- The pairings are then amalgamated into groups of four and pupils are asked to share their findings so far, and then to report back to the whole-class group.
- The tutor's main task in the group discussion and feedback parts of this session will be to ensure that pupils do not strive after consensus so that any similarities and differences emerge clearly.

SESSION 3

Tasks – Different groups of four are set up.
- Pupils are asked now to discuss in their groups and to be prepared to feed back to the whole group on the following question.
- How do the similarities and differences between organisations in terms of:

  - rules
  - what rules are about
  - how rules are communicated
  - the outcome of rule-breaking

  relate to the style and purposes of the different organisations?
  The teacher's task in this discussion and feedback will be:

  - to help pupils explore and clarify any of the relationships which can be found between the style and purposes of organisations and their rules;
  - to help in making a transfer back to the school as an organisation with rules, and in reflecting on the organisation and its rules (leading to a session on what rules the pupils think should be made in schools).

How this activity could be adapted and used

In its present form this activity has a degree of complexity that would be appropriate to the older secondary pupil. Potentially, it raises a series of comparative questions about organisations, their purposes and rules, and how these interrelate, requiring a sophisticated level of analysis to reach deeper understandings. The theme of *Rules in organisations* is, however, one which is relevant to pupils across the age range. It is particularly apt for first-years, who need to come to grips with the secondary school as an organisation in order to feel effective in it. This theme could therefore form a useful part of an induction programme. But in order to work successfully with first-year pupils, modifications would need to be made to the content of this activity (although the suggested format would be equally useful).

The core learning of this theme is that different sorts of organisations tend to have difficult sorts of rules which relate to the purposes and style of these organisations. This leads on to thinking about school rules. To make this activity accessible for first-years, the survey could be reduced to questions *i* to *iv* of Session 1, with corresponding changes in the focused group discussions of Sessions 2 and 3. This could still lead on to the suggested following topic of *Rules in school*. But whereas with older pupils the following sessions would aim to give them an opportunity to explore *their* ideas about what would be useful rules to have in school as a form of consumer survey for the staff, with first-years the aim would be more geared to increasing their skills in the organisation by getting to know the purposes of, and to affiliate to the school rules.

2   Activity – Rules in school – 'The school rules'

Timing This activity would take four linked tutor periods. It would form part of a series on rules in school for first-year pupils as part of an induction programme.
Aim The aim of this activity is for pupils to explore the purposes of rules in school and to examine their own school rules.

SESSION 1

Tasks – The tutor explains the aim of the activity to the pupils.
      – The pupils are asked to say what rules they would suggest for their school.
      – The tutor writes their suggestions on the overhead projector.

- Pupils then work in pairs to think of reasons for the suggested rules, and then share their ideas with the group as a whole.

SESSION 2

Tasks – From the list of rules generated in Session 1 pupils individually select the three rules they think are the most important.
- Pupils then work in small groups to try to reach a consensus on what they consider are the three most important rules, and to discuss the whys and wherefores of their choices.
- In the feedback to the whole class each small group is asked to explain the purposes of their three most important rules, and the reasons why they chose those and rejected others.
- The tutor amends the original list to include all those which the pupils are now proposing as the most important. A tally could be used to indicate the recurring choices.

SESSION 3

Tasks – The tutor presents the pupils' amended selection of rules which were produced in the previous session.
- Pupils recap on the purposes of those rules and the reasons why they chose them.
- The tutor then displays a list of the school's own written rules.
- In groups of four, pupils are asked to examine apparent similiarities and differences in the two sets of rules and to see whether any overlap exists at a deeper level, and then to share their ideas with the class.
- The tutor makes a visual representation of the pupils' findings.

SESSION 4

Tasks – With the visual aid of the conclusions of Session 3, the school's own rules are scrutinised to see if there are any particular rules not represented in the pupils' final list, and to see if there are any of the pupils' proposed rules not represented in the school's list.

– Pupils then work in groups to try to work out:

- the purposes of any school rules which have been identified in this way
- the possible reasons why any of the pupils' rules are not represented in the school's list

and finally the groups share their ideas with the rest of the class.

How this activity could be adapted and used

This activity could also be useful feedback to the organisation. For example, in the pastoral team's review of this series of activities there could be a fruitful discussion on the different tutor groups' conclusions at the end of the final session. This could lead the pastoral team to raise pertinent points regarding school rules for discussion at the school's management level. It could also lead tutors to support first-year school council members in making representations of their views to the school council.

Although this activity, in the form in which it is presented above, is clearly designed with first-years in mind, it could be used in a modified manner for helping pupils at other transitional stages in their school careers to explore possible differences in the school rules and their application. An obvious example for some schools would be as the pupil moves from lower to upper school, or from upper school to sixth form.

It has already been suggested that with older pupils this activity could have a more clearly defined consumer survey purpose. This could be planned into the tutorial programme as a regular feature, providing that the findings were used, and were seen to be used, by the pupils. In this way it could have significant effects in terms of demonstrating the school's responsiveness to the pupils and its willingness to change rules which were redundant or irrelevant to the main purposes of the school.

The informal rules in the school are arguably deserving of more attention than the formal rules by virtue of their complexity, their number and their ubiquitous nature. For the purposes of this book we will deal with the informal rules in operation specifically in classrooms. It is these unwritten rules of the classroom teacher which are more likely to be infringed in the daily life of the average pupil, causing incidents which may be viewed as indiscipline, often leading to underachievement and in some cases to the attribution of deviance (Hargreaves *et al*, 1975). Pupils who are clearly aware of these different sets of informal rules and who are able to spot them in practice will be more skilled in handling themselves in classrooms and in achieving in that setting.

Hargreaves *et al* (1975) identified five separate themes in the teachers' classroom rules. These were talk, movement, time, teacher-pupil and pupil-pupil relationships. All teachers, it seems, have numbers of unwritten rules for managing classroom situations within each of these areas, and this is a fact of classroom life which to some extent is so obvious that it has tended to be taken for granted. We propose that, by encouraging pupils to explore the range and the differences in the informal rules which teachers use, they will feel more certainty about what is expected and will be empowered by the decrease in ambiguity which this brings.

An activity follows which is aimed at increasing pupils' competence in classrooms by encouraging them actively to look for the informal classroom rules used by different teachers. It is, in its present form, geared for use with first-years for the reasons which follow. Most pupils in primary schools tend to have one teacher for the majority of their time in class, although there will be contacts with other adults for different purposes and styles of work. Within a few weeks of starting at a secondary school, however, the same pupil may be handling a dramatic increase in the number of teachers who regularly take the class for lessons (in some schools this can be as high as a seven-fold increase). First-year pupils, therefore, clearly have an urgent need to learn the informal rules of different teachers. And, given the undoubted variations that exist in these informal rules and how they are applied, they also need to learn to respond appropriately and flexibly, as they move from lesson to lesson, to different expectations about their classroom behaviour. By learning at an early stage about the possible variety and range of informal classroom rules, first-year pupils can begin to build up feelings of confidence and competence in themselves as learners in a range of learning situations. The likelihood of lack of success associated with indiscipline, which can lead to disaffection and disaffiliation from school, can therefore be systematically decreased.

3 Activity – Working out different teachers' informal rules for classrooms

Timing This activity would take place over a number of linked tutor periods in the first term of secondary schooling.

Aim The aim of this activity is to help pupils survey the informal rules that teachers use in classrooms so that their competence in these situations is increased.

SESSION 1

Tasks – The tutor clarifies the aims of the activity.

– The tutor explains the difference between the formal school rules, ie the school's written rules, and the informal classroom rules, ie the class teacher's own set of unwritten rules for managing the learning environment.

Examples are provided of the sorts of rules that are commonly found in classrooms such as *Don't talk when the teacher is talking to the whole class*, and of the less common, more idiosyncratic, ones, such as the apocryphal *If you're a new pupil and you go up to the gerbil the teacher will ask you to write about it*.

– Pupils are then asked to think about their last class teacher at primary school and to share with a partner as many of the informal rules that that teacher used as they can think of.

– Pupils feed back to the whole group, with the tutor helping them to appreciate the features in common, and the idiosyncracies of different teachers in the classroom rules they choose to apply.

SESSION 2

Tasks – The tutor helps the group initially to recap the key ideas from the first session of:

i informal classroom rules

ii the range of classroom rules that can be found in terms of commonly found rules and more idiosyncratic rules.

– Pupils explore in groups how they have in their past experience found out what the informal rules of the teacher were.

– The tutor in the feedback helps to elaborate the variety of ways in which informal rules can be detected:

- by noting what is said or done by the teacher in relation to classroom events
- by observing the precursors and consequences of particular actions, inactions, interactions or events in the classroom

- by inferring rules from the teacher's behaviour (verbal and non-verbal).

SESSION 3

Tasks – Following a recap on how the rules can be spotted, the tutor introduces a teacher as a subject for an informal classroom rules inquiry. This could be the tutor her/himself or another teacher who works with first-years and who has high contact time with them.

– Pupils are asked to work in pairs or small groups on the following questions related to the nominated teacher's informal classroom rules. (NB These questions are intended as a stimulus to thinking and discussion and are not in any way an exhaustive list.)

Teachers' informal classroom rules

Equipment

What does this teacher expect you to take to the lesson?

Tick the things the teacher expects you to take and add any others not in the list.

Pencil
Ruler
Rubber
Rough book
Best book
Text book
Coloured pencils
Tippex
Pen, inkpen or biro?
Other items this teacher expects are . . .

Now discuss your ideas and how you worked out what the teacher expects about equipment in lessons.

Work presentation

How does this teacher expect your work to look when you hand it in?

Tick the things the teacher expects and add any others not in the list.

A margin
The heading underlined
Written in pen
Written in pencil
No crossing out
A certain amount of work
Other things this teacher expects are . . .

Now discuss your ideas and how you worked out what the teacher expects about work presentation.

Getting help

How does this teacher expect you to get help when you need it in the lesson?

Tick the things the teacher expects and add any others not in the list.

Put your hand up
Go and ask her/him
Wait until s/he's free
Ask someone else
Go on to the next thing you can do without help
Other ways the teacher expects you to get help are . . .

Now discuss your ideas and the way you worked out how this teacher expects you to get help in lessons.

Homework

What does this teacher expect about homework? How often is it done and when is it handed in?

Tick the things the teacher expects and add any other not in the list.

Homework is set	i every lesson
	ii some lessons
	iii never
	iv once a week
	v any other way?
Homework is handed in	i the next day
	ii the next lesson
	iii by a time set by teacher
	iv in your own time
	v any other way?

Now discuss your ideas and how you worked out what the teacher expects about homework.

Talk

What does this teacher expect about pupils talking in lessons?

Tick the things the teacher expects and add any others not in the list.

Talk at any time providing it's about the work
Talk only in your working group
Talk when you want to get ideas from other pupils
Talk from time to time
Talk when the teacher gives permission
Other times for talk are . . .
Other times for no talk are . . .

Now discuss your ideas and how you worked out what the teacher expects about talk in lessons.

- If the original work was in pairs, groups of four are now formed for pupils to share their ideas so far, followed by feedback to the whole group.
- Using the OHP the tutor makes notes on the pupils' ideas in response on the pupils' ideas in response to the questions, noting any similarities and differences in their ideas. S/he also makes a visual record of their strategies for working out the informal rules.

SESSION 4

Tasks – This session includes (if possible) the teacher who is the subject of the survey as well as the tutor.
– The tutor's task in this session is to help the pupils recap on the ideas they had in the previous session (as noted on the OHP) about this teacher's informal classroom rules, and the strategies they had used for identifying them. Any new ideas that have occurred to pupils in the interim are added. The teacher helps by commenting from his/her perspective on their ideas about the informal rules s/he uses and by clarifying any issues about informal rules when there is uncertainty. Both the tutor and the teacher contribute towards helping pupils elaborate their detection strategies and their ideas.

SESSIONS 5 AND 6

Tasks – Pupils are asked to repeat the tasks of Session 3 with other teachers in mind. Groups of pupils can work on different teachers or the whole group on the same one. The aim is similar in each case: to identify different teachers' informal classroom rules and to elaborate strategies for detecting them.
   – In the feedback the tutor helps pupils develop their ideas on identification and detection and note important variations between teachers.

How this activity could be adapted and used

This can be a useful style of activity to develop at various times over a pupil's school career, with more complex ideas about informal classroom rules introduced progressively. Hargreaves' five themes of talk, movement, time, teacher–pupil and pupil–pupil relationships, referred to earlier in this chapter, are in themselves, and without further elaboration, useful structuring devices. These could be introduced at quite an early stage as a way of focusing on particular aspects of informal rules, and subsequently developed. Further, Hargreaves' notion of the phases of a lesson – entry, settling down to tasks, changing tasks, finishing off tasks, packing up and leaving (each of which has a different combination of informal rules) – can also be useful in structuring a more detailed investigation. It would be particularly appropriate to introduce this activity at phases of transition, when a pupil was about to meet new sets of teachers, for example when starting new options or when moving into the sixth form, as well as at the time of first-year induction. However, we do feel that this activity has application more frequently if pupils are to develop elaborated ideas about how classrooms work, so that they have more skills available to them as participants in those settings, and we would therefore advocate a more regular use.

This activity also provides teachers with some interesting data about pupils' perceptions of their informal classroom rules and how they are conveyed. Teachers may find this invaluable in reviewing their own practice in terms of the informal rules they are using (or are viewed as using by their pupils), what their rationales are for these rules, and whether these are in fact the rules they intend to convey. They can also take the opportunity to consider whether the rules that are conveyed are the ones best suited to their purposes within the classroom. For example, a teacher may discover that pupils have detected a rule related to talk, which from that teacher's perspective reduces the amount and/or style of talk which is needed in that lesson in order to process, assimilate, and therefore learn effectively. This focus on informal classroom rules could be taken up as a form of enquiry for teachers to view and develop the learning process in their classrooms. In this way teachers can begin to consider in what ways they are conveying to pupils the informal rules and the extent to which they may need to be more explicit about them. This would be no 'simple' exercise aimed at creating a false notion of consensus between teachers on such important aspects of classroom life: it would, on the contrary, provide a valuable arena for reflecting on and considering how individual teachers, supported by teacher colleagues, could extend their knowledge about themselves and their pupil's experience of learning.

At this point we will conclude our suggestions for activities. By taking as our example the sometimes apparently unexciting theme of rules in school, we hope to have shown that tutorial activities can be developed so that they actively examine centrally important aspects of school life. We also intend to suggest that the outcomes of tutorial programmes will not be limited to pupil learning, but will also involve teacher learnings and sometimes organisational change.

Tutorial programmes which operate as part of a well planned pastoral curriculum in a responsive school system can generate lively and powerful learning. However as an isolated ingredient in a rigid environment they can degenerate to moralising, which is both ineffective and can led to pupil disaffiliation.

It follows that the pastoral team, perhaps as a result of tutorial work on such themes, will be concerned to examine wider features of the school's responsiveness. This will form part of the team's concern about numerous features of the school ethos and its effect on pupil learning (but perhaps everyone's response-ability is involved here). The degree to which self control as opposed to external control is encouraged in pupils, the degree to which pupils are encouraged to take responsibility and participate in the school decision-making: these are major considerations which have influence on patterns of discipline and are in need of attention as part of the pastoral team's long-term contribution.

Lest these suggestions sound like some sort of 'split' where the pastoral team is charged with putting everyone else's house in order, we now turn to examine the team's own management of its activities. This is another area where its long-term contribution to patterns of discipline may be examined.

Pastoral effects through the pastoral management

It is probably the case that the pastoral system of a school has its effects through a complex combination of interpersonal processes, mainly between pupils and tutors. In this way it is similar to schools at large and to classrooms in particular. And it is also similar in that the effects generated can be any of a diverse range, some positive and some negative.

One of the major tasks in managing the pastoral system is that of keeping its particular ethos headed in a constructive and creative direction. This will involve giving attention to the way it is portrayed, perceived and used, with an associated attention focusing on the roles of staff who carry responsibility for various aspects of the pastoral task.

In this section some of the considerations for keeping the pastoral system's approach to school discipline a creative one will be outlined. This will not of course cover all aspects of management. With the particular focus of this book, we shall examine:

1 the purpose of the pastoral system
2 the portrayal of the pastoral system
3 the roles in the pastoral system
4 the development in the pastoral system

1 The purpose of the pastoral system

It is perhaps unnecessary to state that the purpose of the pastoral system is not that of sorting out discipline problems. Yet this distorted practice is all too often encountered in schools and is taken to be the purpose by some people outside schools, including some parents, some educational administrators, and the occasional sociologist of education.

Happily, it is nowadays more accepted that such practice is easily seen to be ineffective. As Pik (1981) has observed 'the least effective pastoral care teams I have encountered are those that are construed by the staff as dealing exclusively with discipline problems, ie handing out punishment to "troublemakers" sent to them by class teachers and form teachers.'

In moving away from this style of practice the question of the purpose of pastoral care can be profitably raised, especially as on some occasions staff seem to be saying, 'If we give up dealing with naughty pupils what shall we do?'

The most effective pastoral care is clearly related to the major goals of the school – the intellectual and social development of all young people.

In this style the pastoral task is not directed toward a minority of pupils: the personal-social dimension of getting the most out of school is taken seriously for all pupils, and the pastoral effort has a dual focus – encouraging, supporting and offering guidance for an extensive range of pupil achievement in and out of school, alongside the development of a responsive staff and school system. In this manner pastoral care develops an expertise in understanding the pupil's experience of school, in order to modify things for greater success, and therefore does not operate at the expense of understanding the teacher's experience of school. It follows that when pastoral care is operating at its best, many of the divisions which are talked about can be seen to be spurious. Pastoral staff have no monopoly on caring (despite the unfortunate title), nor is it realistic to portray the others (whoever they may be) by contrast as the ones who are either exercising control or in control. The challenge to integrate creatively care and control in the service of pupils' development is the challenge for the pastoral system, as it is for every classroom and other aspect of school. Similarly, the division of 'pastoral problems' (to be referred to year tutor) and 'discipline problems' (to be referred to head of subject department) is clearly confusing and unworkable. Many of the examples of dividing pastoral and academic issues are similarly spurious, and do not obtain in effective school systems.

However, to argue that effective pastoral care is that which does not operate in a divided manner should not be confused with any attempt to argue that divisions are necessarily generated by the existence of posts with special responsibility. On the contrary, our present forms of organisation of the secondary school hold such potential for fragmentation that special posts are understandably necessary to facilitate an integrated perspective on pupil's experience. In effective school systems it is not the case that role specialisation (such as the existence of year tutors) necessarily leads to role segregation.

If we take the major goals of a school's pastoral system to be:

a providing a personal point of contact for every pupil and his/her parents
b offering support and guidance for pupil achievement and development (including personal-social development)
c monitoring pupil progress and performance across the whole school
d providing colleagues with information to adapt teaching, and promoting a responsive school system,

it follows that the pastoral system will have a concern about disruptive behaviour (on the part of the pupil as well as on the part of the school), but it does not follow that the pastoral system would necessarily have more of a concern or responsibility for disruptive behaviour than any other aspect of the total school system. From this perspective it is very plain what a distortion the 'discipline fixation' of some pastoral systems represents, and also what else is being omitted.

2   The portrayal of the pastoral system

The purposes of any school's pastoral system are not self-evident and are not achieved by analysis alone. Rather, they are brought into life in day-to-day communication, both the formal and the informal. This is why it is important for management to pay attention to how the pastoral activity is portrayed.

If the pastoral system is consistently portrayed along the lines of the goals listed above, to pupils, parents, all staff and others, a creative approach to school discipline will be communicated as a part. On the other hand, if pupils get the impression of year tutors as 'hatchet people', if parents get the sense that they hear from the pastoral staff only when there's 'trouble', and if subject teachers pick up the view that someone else will cope with classroom problems, then the pastoral system will soon find itself with numerous 'discipline problems' waiting at its door.

Communicating a positive and integrated view of discipline within pastoral care is a task which needs continued attention. There are real forces which work against an integrated view, and the danger that the system will revert to a distorted style of functioning is continually present in the stressful context of the secondary school. The immediacy of 'problems', and the associated calls for action to be taken, can easily start to take time away from the longer-term tasks and priorities in pastoral care, and a short-term, demand-led style of crisis management and problem focus can soon return.

Therefore, those with a wish to maintain a more positive view of pastoral care will need practice in not responding to attempts to off-load responsibility for minor crises. Skills of assertiveness are required to communicate to a colleague that his/her request is inappropriate. It is all too easy to be pressurised into action as though the most immediate demands should take the highest priority. On occasions it will be clear that colleagues do not like it if the pastoral system does not respond in the way they wish, and on such occasions tutors will need to resist the pressures of their peer group toward individualising the 'problem', and consequently taking it on board.

The preceding points apply to informal day-to-day communication between staff, but the formal aspects of communication also need monitoring for their portrayal of the pastoral system. School brochures and handbooks, staff analysis and role descriptions, advertisements for posts and announcements for events – all these written forms have potential for conveying an image of pastoral care. We hope that it will not be too long before every school understands the negative implications in advertising for a year tutor 'to be responsible for the discipline and welfare of 200 pupils'!

3   The roles in the pastoral system

If purposes have been clarified, and the portrayal of them is approximately right, then we have supportive ingredients for a central task of management – ensuring that the various roles and role relationships are enacted in a correspondingly creative way and do not slip back into any of the available distortions.

The most fundamental and central role in any pastoral system is that of the form tutor. Over the past decade this statement has been more widely accepted as important (rather than a hopeful ideal), even though some schools have not yet made the organisational rearrangements necessary for the statement to be realised. The form tutor is the point of first contact, who offers first-line support and guidance and who creates an overview of each pupil's progress and performance. It is the form tutor who has important knowledge of the pupil and who is therefore, crucial in communications with pupils, parents, teachers and others. To exercise such a role effectively requires that resources are available for the role – resources of time, channels of communication and support. In schools where these resources are not made available the pastoral system does not deserve such a title – it is generally empty from its core, and overworked year tutors use their energies ineffectively.

With regard to matters of discipline, the form tutor's role is never likely to be one of providing immediate support on all occasions of classroom deviance – that is all to the good, ultimately. But the form tutor's overview of pupils' performance will incorporate the occurrences of classroom difficulties, and it is therefore more appropriate that the form tutor is consulted periodically rather than immediately. In these circumstances the tutor's advice or information about a pupil can be constructively utilised, without an off-loading sort of referral taking place. Galloway's (1983) analyses of four secondary schools with particularly low reported incidence of disruptive behaviour, suggested that the form tutor was used in such a way in these schools, whereas in another ten schools this use was defeated by lack of a policy of continuity of tutors, lack of time to meet the tutor group, and a lack of teaching contact between tutor and tutor group.

Turning our attention to another major role in the pastoral system, the head of year/house/section, it will be by now fairly clear that if this role is exercised as though it offered a major contribution to solving immediate problems of classroom indiscipline, then a distorted and ineffective pastoral system may result. Reynolds and Murgatroyd (1977) report a study of 76 schools where the stated responsibility for dealing with problems – in their example, truancy – was investigated. There was an association between the dealing with problems by middle and senior management (at the expense of the form tutors) and the seriousness of the perceived problem: dealing with problems at middle-management level was associated with higher levels of perceived problem. We cannot, of course, directly infer a simple causal connection between these observations of the type *Year tutors' dealing with problems increases problems*. But it is more reasonable to conclude that in schools where problems are referred up to year tutors there is no evidence that the problems are solved more effectively than in schools which do not adopt this practice.

It is more realistic and more effective to view the head of year/house/section as mainly a team leader rather than mainly a super problem-solver. From this perspective we can recognise the major tasks of the role as facilitating and supporting the work of the tutors, monitoring various aspects of the year or house group, communicating and facilitating tutors' communication with all concerned: pupils, parents, staff and others. Considerations of discipline are therefore a special case of this general picture. We would expect to see team leaders using their extra time to initiate monitoring, to organise and facilitate relevant meetings between relevant persons, to take an active part in all aspects of policy making, planning and delivering the curriculum as a whole. The practical strategies which have been advocated in earlier chapters of this book have been examples of this perspective: they involve collecting information and facilitating the use of that information amongst a relevant group. In this way 'discipline' does not become a separated, crisis concern, but is one part of the longer-term focus of the pastoral team, its curriculum offer and its management. An additional result would be that the over-talked-about 'pastoral-academic split' is seen to be another false divide, since each of the teacher teams in an effective school system can see its particular contribution to the shared overall goal. On the occasions when there has been partial evidence for such a split, it has been mainly attributable to a lack of communication at the middle-management level between the various team leaders, especially the leaders of pastoral teams and subject teams. On these occasions each has underplayed the aspect of their role which requires them to engage in extensive communication with each other.

A final point is worth making on the relationship between form tutor and team leader. Where the team leader has extra time resources to fulfil their responsibilities, there may be occasions when a form tutor requests that the team leader contribute to a particular task by taking on some part of it. This could include a request to work with an individual member of the tutor group. In the particular area of discipline, such a request would not constitute an off-loading sort of referral, but would comprise a carefully thought out occasion when the team leader with the skill, time, and credibility could offer help to a particular member of the tutor group.

4 The development of the pastoral system

The previous sections have set some part of the agenda for the long-term development of a pastoral care system whose contribution to school discipline is a creative one. There are a few further comments worth making.

Management of a pastoral system includes giving time to thinking about the system's performance and development. It includes thinking ahead, both to develop the system and to anticipate future changes. Therefore, a system which has a regular practice of reviewing its performance and its contribution to the school at large will be in a more powerful position both to initiate change and to respond to change. Reviewing is a central process in all sorts of learning and is particularly important in successful school-based development. It need not be taken as something complicated or formalised: it may simply mean that some time is given so that a tutor team can sit down with its leader and address such topics as: what we have achieved, what we find most successful, what we would like to be different, and what we need in order to develop. Such conversations can lead effectively into other important processes such as the identification of tutors' INSET needs and other elements in the overall picture of staff development. They can also lead into elements of system development, in that (especially if they have available the results of various monitoring activities which have been undertaken) they constitute an important ingredient of evaluation (other ingredients such as the perspectives of pupils and parents would need to be added).

On the particular topic of discipline the strategies advocated in this book have aimed to set off in part these processes of evaluation and

themes. Take the themes suggested for the pastoral curriculum of: the bodily self; the sexual self; the social self; the vocational self; the moral/political self; the self as a learner; the organisational self.

a Discuss how one of these themes could be used to organise the content of a learning offer within the pastoral curriculum.

b Elaborate the possible content of the theme.

c Identify areas of overlap with other themes.

d Discuss where aspects of the theme could possibly be located (having in mind possible overlap) eg tutorial programmes, specialist guidance lessons, subject lessons, etc.

2 The aim of this topic is to examine the inter-relation between important themes in the tutorial programme, and in the activities which may raise those themes.

Take the following themes which could be addressed through inter-relating activities within the tutorial programme:

i skills for effective study

ii attitudes to learning; self as a learner; relationships with peers in learning situations; teacher styles and expectations; parental expectations with regard to learning and schooling; self in relation to the school as an organisation; rules in school.

Taking *i* and any two others from those listed at *ii* discuss the sorts of activities you would include in a tutorial programme to address each. Examine the themes and the content of the activities for their inter-relation.

3 The aim of this discussion topic is to develop thinking about informal school rules and the skills of adapting and modifying published materials to meet the needs of the school and the pupils.

Take the activity on *Informal school rules* and discuss how this could be developed for use with a more senior group of pupils.

Try out the amended activity (at least two members of the discussion group).

Report back to the discussion group and make further adaptations on the basis of the try-out.

4 The aim of this discussion topic is to develop ideas on possible changes in the school rules.

a Duplicate a copy of the school rules for each member of the pastoral team. Then consider the rules on the following dimensions. Are they:

– clearly stated?

– easily enforceable?

– the minimum number possible?

– reasonable and meaningful (to the pupil)?

b Discuss how in your school you could survey pupils' views on the
school rules.

Pastoral management

1 How would you describe the present relationship between discipline
issues and pastoral care in your school – solely short-term crisis
management? Some medium-term reflection and monitoring? Some
long-term preventative work?

　In your discussion group identify the forces and pressures in your
school which play a part in generating and maintaining the present
picture.

　If your pastoral team is seeking to create a change in the picture,
what would you choose as the forces and pressures which first require
modification?
2 Examine the goals for a pastoral system which are outlined on p 159.

　Give your estimate of the proportion of the pastoral team's time
which is spent on each of the four main areas listed.

　What has been left out and what proportion of the pastoral team's
time do you estimate is spent on these activities?

　Discuss how much time is presently devoted to various aspects
(short, medium and long-term) of discipline issues.

　What will need to change for this overall picture to change?
Identify in detail particular practices and personnel. What extra
skills/support/resources will the pastoral team need?

　How will you disseminate the estimates you have arrived at?
3 Collect together all the documents in which the school makes some
statement about its pastoral system. What is the picture of pastoral
case which is portrayed? What is the implied role with regard to
discipline matters?

　If your discussion group or your pastoral team wishes to change the
overall picture,
　– identify the statements which need change, the mechanism through
　　which they may be modified, and draft your preferred version,
　– assess the degree to which these statements affect the daily picture
　　in school life, and the mechanisms through which this effect occurs.
　　What practices will need to change for any new statements to take
　　positive effect?
4 Discuss the role of the form tutor as it operates in your school, and
compare with the comments on p 161. Are the major goals of contact,
overview and guidance supported by the resources of time, communication channels and back-up?

Now examine the aspects of the form tutor's role which are devoted to discipline matters. Is their knowledge of pupils appropriately engaged on such occasions? Or is their role more one of handing out detentions?

Identify all of the aspects which will need to change if you consider the role of form tutor should be developed (ie goals, tasks, skills and resources of tutor and of the various role-partners). Arrange these aspects in terms of their importance in the change you plan. Devise a detailed programme for change, making sure it is built on a realistic time-scale (for example, three years for a significant role change overall).

5 Discuss the role of the pastoral team leader as it operates in your school, and compare with the brief comments on p 162. Are the major goals of facilitating tutors, monitoring, and communicating supported by effective use of meetings and access to policy-making?

Examine the aspects of the team leader's role which relate to discipline matters, and assess whether the role is presently operated in an effective manner on such issues.

Identify all of the aspects which will need to change if the role of the pastoral team leader needs to change (ie goals, tasks, skills and resources of that role and its various role partners). Arrange these aspects in terms of their importance in the change you plan. Devise a detailed programme for change, making sure it is built on a realistic time-scale.

6 Examine the processes which are available in your school for a pastoral team to review its work.

Draw up a plan for a review meeting in a pastoral team.

Devote attention to the timing, venue, and resources (including refreshments) for such a meeting.

What structure will you use for the meeting (structures of timing, discussion structures, recording and facilitating)?

What stimulus will you use for the meeting?

What themes will you address in the meeting? (Will any of the above discussion suggestions be of use?)

What information may the meeting need?

How may meetings for review become a regular feature of your practice?

Bibliography

Amphlett, D., Davies, J. and Jones, D. (1985) *In the Heat of the Moment* – videotape, Oxford Polytechnic Press.

Bales, R.F. (1970) *Personality and Interpersonal Behaviour*, Holt, Rinehart and Winston.

Ball, S.J. (1981) *Beachside Comprehensive: a case study of secondary schooling*, Cambridge University Press.

Barker, R.G. (1963) 'On the nature of the environment', *Journal of Social Issues*, 19:4, 17–38.

Bell, L. and Maher, P. (1986) *Leading a Pastoral Team*, Blackwell.

Bird, C. (1980) 'Deviant labelling in school: the pupils' perspective' in Woods, P. (ed) *Pupil Strategies*, Croom Helm.

Bird, C., Chessum, R., Furlong, J. and Johnson, D. (1980) *Disaffected Pupils*, Brunel University, Educational Studies Unit.

Cannan, C. (1970) 'Schools for delinquency' *New Society*, 16:427, 1004.

Chapman, B.L.M. (1979) 'Schools do make a difference', *British Educational Research Journal*, 5:1, 115–24.

Chessum, R. (1980) 'Teacher ideologies and pupil disaffection' in Barton, L., Meighan, R. and Walker, S. (eds), *Schooling, Ideology and the Curriculum*, Falmer Press.

Clarke, D.D. (1981) 'Disruptive incidents in secondary school classrooms: a sequence analysis approach', *Oxford Review of Education*, 7:2, 111–17.

Coffield, F., Borrill, C. and Marshall, S. (1986) *Growing Up at the Margins*, Open University Press.

Corrie, M., Haystead, J. and Zaklukiewicz, S. (1982) *Classroom Management Strategies; a study in secondary schools*, Hodder and Stoughton.

Daines, R. (1981) 'Withdrawal units and the psychology of problem behaviour' in Gillham, B. (ed) *Problem Behaviour in Secondary Schools*, Croom Helm.

Davie, R., Butler, N. and Goldstein, H. (1972) *From Birth to Seven*, Longman.

168

Davies, L. (1979) 'Deadlier than the Male? Girls' conformity and deviance in school' in Barton, L. and Meighan, R. (eds) *Schools, Pupils, and Deviance*, Nafferton Books.

Davies, L. (1984) *Pupil Power: deviance and gender at school*, Falmer Press.

Dierenfield, R.B. (1982). (1982) *Classroom Disruption in English Comprehensive Schools*, Macalester College Education Dept, St Paul, Minnesota. (see *Times Educational Supplement*, 29.1.82, p 4)

Doyle, W. (1979) 'Making managerial decisions in classrooms' in Duke, D.L. (ed) *Classroom Mangement*, University of Chicago Press.

Doyle, W. (1980) *Classroom Management*, Kappa Delta Pi.

Epstein, J.L. (ed) (1981) *The Quality of School Life*, Lexington Books.

Fox, R., Luszki, M.B. and Schmuck, R. (1966) *Diagnosing Classroom Learning Environments*, Science Research Associates.

Fuller, M. (1982) 'Young, female and black' in Cashmore, R. and Troyna, B. (eds) *Black Youth in Crisis*, George Allen and Unwin.

Furlong, V.J. (1976) 'Interaction sets in the classroom' in Stubbs, M. and Delamont, S. (eds) *Explorations in Classroom Observation*, Wiley.

Furlong, V.J. (1984) 'Black resistance in the liberal comprehensive' in Delamont, S. (ed) *Readings on interaction in the classroom*, Methuen.

Galloway, D. (1983) 'Disruptive pupils and effective pastoral care' *School Organisation*, 3:3, 245–254.

Galloway, D., Ball, T., Bloomfield, D. and Seyd, R. (1982) *Schools and Disruptive Pupils*, Longman.

Gannaway, H. (1976) 'Making sense of school' in Stubbs, M. and Delamont, S. (eds) *Explorations in Classroom Observation*, Wiley.

Georgiades, N. and Phillimore, L. (1975) 'The myth of the hero-innovator, and alternative strategies for organisational change' in Kiernan, C.C. and Woodford, F.P. (eds) *Behaviour Modification with the Severely Retarded*, Associated Scientific Publishers, also reprinted in Easen, P. (1985) *Making School-Centred INSET Work*, Open University Press.

Gillham, B. (1984) 'School organisation and the control of disruptive incidents' in Frude, N. and Gault, H. (eds) *Disruptive Behaviour in Schools*, Wiley.

Graham, P. and Rutter, M. (1970) 'Selection of children with psychiatric disorders' in Rutter, M., Tizard, J. and Whitmore, K. (eds) *Education, Health and Behaviour*, Longman.

Hamblin, D.H. (1974) *The Teacher and Counselling*, Blackwell.

Hamblin, D.H. (1978) *The Teacher and Pastoral Care*, Blackwell.

Hamblin, D.H. (1981) *Teaching Study Skills*, Blackwell.

Hamblin, D.H. (1984) *Pastoral Care In-Service Training Manual*, Blackwell.

Hamblin, D.H. (1986) 'The failure of pastoral care?' *School Organisation*, 6:1, 141–8.

Handy, C. (1984) *Taken for Granted? Understanding schools as organisations*, Longman/Schools Council.

Hargreaves, D.H. (1967) *Social Relations in a Secondary School*, Routledge and Kegan Paul.

Hargreaves, D.H. (1975) *Interpersonal Relations and Education*, revised edition, Routledge and Kegan Paul.

Hargreaves, D.H. (1979) 'Durkheim, deviance and education' in Barton, L. and Meighan, R. (eds) *Schools, Pupils and Deviance*, Nafferton Books.

Hargreaves, D.H. (1980) 'Teachers' knowledge of behaviour problems' in Upton, G. and Gobell, A. (eds) *Behaviour Problems in the Comprehensive School*, University College Cardiff Faculty of Education.

Hargreaves, D.H. (1982) *The Challenge for the Comprehensive School*, Routledge and Kegan Paul.

Hargreaves, D.H., Hester, S.K. and Mellor, F.J. (1975) *Deviance in Classrooms*, Routledge and Kegan Paul.

Her Majesty's Inspectorate (1984) *Education Observed 2*, DES.

ILEA (1982) *Sex Differences and Achievement*, Research and Statistics publication 823/82.

ILEA (1984) *Improving Secondary Schools*, ILEA.

ILEA (1984) *Improving Secondary Schools: Research Studies*, ILEA.

Jackson, P.W. (1968) *Life in Classrooms*, Holt, Rinehart and Winston.

Johnson, D. and Ransom, E. (1983) *Family and School*, Croom Helm.

Jones, A. (1984) 'Studying school effectiveness: a postscript' in Reynolds, D. (ed) *Studying School Effectiveness*, Falmer Press.

Kounin, J.S. (1976) *Discipline and Group Management in Classrooms*, Holt, Rinehart and Winston.

Lacey, C. (1970) *Hightown Grammar*, Manchester University Press.

Lawrence, J., Steed, D. and Young, P. (1977) *Disruptive Behaviour in a Secondary School*, Educational Studies Monograph No 1, University of London Goldsmiths College.

Lawrence, J., Steed, D. and Young, P. (1981) *Dialogue on Disruptive Behaviour*, PJD Press.

Lawrence, J., Steed, D. and Young, P. (1984) *Disruptive Children – Disruptive Schools?*, Croom Helm.

McRobbie, A. and Garber, J. (1976) 'Girls and subcultures' in Hall, S. and Jefferson, T. (eds) *Resistance through Rituals*, Hutchinson.

Marsh, P., Rosser, E. and Harre, R. (1978) *The Rules of Disorder*, Routledge and Kegan Paul.

Martin, W.B.W. (1975) *The Negotiated Order of the School*, MacMillan of Canada.

Meyenn, R. (1980) 'Schoolgirls' peer groups' in Woods, P. (ed) *Pupil Strategies*, Croom Helm.

Mortimore, P. (1980) 'Misbehaviour in Schools' in Upton, G. and Gobell, A. (eds) *Behaviour Problems in the Comprehensive School*, Faculty of Education, University College Cardiff.

Pik, R. (1981) 'Confrontation situations and teacher support sysems' in Gillham, B. (ed) *Problem Behaviour in the Secondary School*, Croom Helm.

Power, M.J., Alderson, M.R., Phillipson, C.M., Schoenberg, E. and Morris, J.M. (1967) 'Delinquent Schools' *New Society*, 19.10.67, 10, 542–3.

Rabinowitz, A. (1981) 'The range of solutions: a critical analysis' in Gillham, B. (ed) *Problem Behaviour in Secondary Schools*, Croom Helm.

Reynolds, D. (1976) 'When teachers and pupils refuse a truce: the secondary school and the creation of delinquency' in Mungham, G. and Pearson, G. (eds) *Working Class Youth Cultures*, Routledge and Kegan Paul.

Reynolds, D. (1977) 'Towards a socio-psychological view of truancy' in Kahan, B. (ed) *Working Together for Children and their families*, HMSO.

Reynolds, D. and Murgatroyd, S. (1977) 'The sociology of schooling and the absent pupil: the school as a factor in the generation of truancy' in Carroll, H.C.M. (ed) *Absenteeism in South Wales*, University College Swansea Faculty of Education.

Rutter, M., Maughan, B., Mortimore, P. and Ousten, J. (1979) *Fifteen Thousand Hours: secondary schools and their effects on children*, Open Books.

Schmuck, R. and Schmuck, P.A. (1979) *Group Processes in the Classroom*, W.C. Brown.

Stebbins, R. (1976) *Teachers and Meaning*, E.J. Brill.

Steed, D. (1983) '"Tired of school": Danish disruptive pupils and ours', *Cambridge Journal of Education*, 12:1, 20–25.

Steed, D., Lawrence, J. and Young, P. (1983) 'Beyond the naughty child', *Times Educational Supplement*, 28.10.83.

Steedman, J. (1980) *Progress in Secondary Schools*, National Children's Bureau.

Sykes, G.M. and Matza, D. (1957) 'Techniques for neutralising deviant identity', *American Sociological Review*, 22, 557–670, also in Rubington, E. and Weinberg, M.S. (eds) (1973) *Deviance: the Interactionist Perspective*, Macmillan.

Tattum, D. (1982) *Disruptive Pupils in Schools and Units*, Wiley.

Tattum, D. (1985) 'Control and welfare: towards a theory of

constructive discipline in schools' in Ribbins, P. (ed) *Schooling and Welfare*, Falmer Press.

Tattum, D. (ed) (1986) *Management of Disruptive Pupil Behaviour in Schools*, Wiley.

Tomlinson, M. (1986) *National Priorities for In-Service Training*, SCETT conference (reported *Times Educational Supplement*, July 1986).

Underwood Committee (1955) *Report of the Committee on Maladjusted Behaviour*, HMSO.

Walden, R. and Walkerdine, V. (1985) *Girls and Mathematics*, Bedford Way Papers, No 24, University of London Institute of Education.

Watkins, C. (1981) 'Adolescents and Activities' in Hamblin, D.H. (ed) *Problems and Practice of Pastoral Care*, Blackwell.

Watkins, C. (1985) 'Does pastoral care = personal and social education?' *Pastoral Care in Education*, 3:3, 179–183.

Watkins, C. (1986) 'Managing pastoral classrooms', paper to NAPCE annual conference – Managing the Pastoral Process.

Wall, W.D. (1974) *Constructive Education for Adolescents*, Harrap/ UNESCO.

Wedell, K. and Lindsay, G.A. (1980) 'Early identification procedures: what have we learned?' *Remedial Education*, 15:3, 130–135.

Willis, P. (1977) *Learning to Labour: how working class kids get working class jobs*, Saxon House.

Woods, P. (1979) *The Divided School*, Routledge and Kegan Paul.

Index

review. When they are successful, they will contribute towards that crucial feature of any school which is coping well with discipline – an atmosphere in which teachers find it possible to talk about and receive relevant help on teaching. In such an atmosphere, where the connected features of the pupils' personal intellectual and social development are addressed, we believe it likely that a maximum number of pupils will get a maximum amount from their school career. It is towards the maintenance and development of such an atmosphere that we hope this volume may contribute.

Summary

This chapter has examined the long-term role of pastoral care in its relationship to school discipline. Two main sections have been covered: the whole-school pastoral curriculum in its pro-active and preventative aspects toward school discipline, and the pastoral management in its positive and creative stance on school discipline.

The pastoral curriculum was analysed as a planned and co-ordinated learning offer for all pupils, promoting social-personal development with respect to pupils at school, in the community and in later life. Tutorial programmes are but one of the locations of the pastoral curriculum, albeit one which is specially characterised by the tutor's extra knowledge of and relationship with the tutor group. Of the themes connected with school discipline which might be addressed in tutorial programmes, this chapter has developed *Rules in school* in some depth, with suggested activities and their development.

The pastoral management was analysed in terms of its purpose, its portrayal, its roles, and its development. In each, some of the issues were raised for maintaining a creative approach to discipline by the pastoral team. Some of the possible difficulties, which might be experienced when resisting the short-term crisis view of pastoral care, were anticipated. There is no substitute for a system which incorporates well-resourced form tutors, skilled team leaders and regular review.

Suggestions for discussion/investigation

Pastoral Curriculum

1 The aim of this topic is that the pastoral team identify preventative aspects of the pastoral curriculum through a structured set of